THE Beer lover's GUIDE TO VINTAGE ADVERTISING

featuring hundreds of classic **beer, ale & lager** ads from American history

BEER, FROM THE REVOLUTION THROUGH PROHIBITION

BY NANCY J. PRICE

The Beer Lover's Guide to Vintage Advertising: Featuring Hundreds of Classic Beer, Ale & Lager Ads from American History

synchronista

THE Beer lover's GUIDE TO VINTAGE ADVERTISING

featuring hundreds of classic beer, ale & lager ads from American history

BEER, FROM THE REVOLUTION THROUGH PROHIBITION

A chapter of beer history

The American people have been a drinking nation from the time of the first settlement of this country.

The Puritan settlers of New England used beer as their daily beverage, their ingenuity having invented a fermented liquor resembling beer, which was brewed out of "pumpkins, parsnips, and walnut-tree chips." Later malt and hops were substituted, and the manufacture and sale of malt liquors was encouraged.

As early as 1641 was the cultivation of hops introduced in the Massachusetts colony, and the first malt-house was erected in the same year.

Prior to 1667, the New England legislature passed a law that "beer should be made with four bushels of good barley malt at least to a hogshead, without any mixture of molasses, cane sugar, or other materials instead of malt, and that it should not sold above two pence the quart."

In Pennsylvania the manufacture of beer was commenced as early as 1683, under the direction of the founder and proprietor of the colony — William Penn, who subsequently erected a malt-house and brewery near his residence at Pennsbury, along the Delaware river.

It thus appears that the manufacture of malt liquors was encouraged at an early date in the history of this country.

Washington and Franklin are both known to have been fond of their beer and wine, as there are numerous instances extant of their indulgence in their favorite beverages. The lives of such men as Hamilton, Jefferson, Madison, Morris, Gates, Green and others could be cited as examples of prominent individuals in the early history of this country who favored the use of malt and other liquors.

It is accordingly evident that what the greatest statesmen of this country practised cannot be morally wrong; and it is, therefore, an excess of legislative power to make the sale of malt and spirituous liquors a statutory crime, as is desired by prohibitionists.

- As published in *The Reading Times* (Pennsylvania) on June 7, 1878

A toast to the past

Welcome, beer lovers, to a time when the brew wasn't only something to be enjoyed, but was actually celebrated as a healthy drink that sparked the appetite and helped you sleep.

Beer has been made and sold in this country since before it even *was* a country. In fact, as far back as the 1600s, Manhattan (then known as New Amsterdam) was home to some of the first commercial breweries this side of the Atlantic. Still, it took more than a hundred years before companies regularly advertised their wares.

We dove deep into newspaper archives to find hundreds of early ads for beers and brewers — covering the years between the American Revolution and the end of Prohibition — then put them all together to make this picture of the past. With more than 400 individual clippings, hundreds of vintage beer brands are represented! (We have also included a comprehensive index, which starts on page 176.)

> *"A continuous round of pleasure, as well as perpetual good health, is assured"*

Inside, you will see that beer advertisements in the 18th century were often little more than polite invitations to the locals and passing ship captains. In the 19th century, every brand was "celebrated" and "the best" — while some promotional posters showed creepy caricatures loving their drinks maybe a little *too* much.

Advertisers of the 20th century built upon all of those concepts, then added their own spin, slipping in buzzwords like "purity" and "cleanliness," "nourishment" and "food value."

All of the authentic antique images in this book were carefully chosen, then digitally restored as much as possible to return them to their original glory. Ads are presented in sections based on the date of publication, so you can easily find a specific era, or simply browse the ads to see how trends and techniques changed through the years.

So grab a bottle of your favorite malted beverage, and enjoy this little trip back through time. As they used to say, "After the nervous tension of a day's work, there's no better relaxation than a glass of good beer." Or a *book* about good beer.

Cheers!

Nancy J. Price
Founder, Click Americana (ClickAmericana.com)
... and great-granddaughter of a Master Brewer

This collection of more than 400 ads covers more than a century and a half of American beer marketing. Aside from the historical value, it's hard not to be amused by — or hit by the absurdity of — many of the promotional tactics that worked well all those years ago.

Want some examples? Here are a few of our favorite lines:

1. "When the patient is weak, the doctor says 'Drink beer.'"
2. "The true health food beverage."
3. "Blatz beer... it's my *very best friend*."
4. "A beverage you may offer your wife."
5. "The foundation of a happy household."
6. "Why drink water when you can get Salem beer?"
7. "Quickly dispels fatigue, invigorates, and refreshes."
8. "A glass or two at noon brightens the lunch hour."
9. "A bottle of Schlitz at bedtime means sound, beneficial sleep."
10. "Have a good time — it makes you a better man for the next day's work."

Are you looking for something specific?

Check out the index starting on page 176

— Other notes —

The antique and vintage advertisements in this book have been restored as faithfully as possible, but in most cases, we relied upon high-resolution scans of the printed newspaper and magazine pages. As such, some details have been lost due to printing processes, environmental damage, and issues with the quality of preserved paper, microfiche, negatives and scans.

Overall, the book is organized chronologically. However, within each section (year, decade or century, denoted by the white on black marker on one of the outer edges of each page), the advertisements are not arranged by date, but were formatted based on content and for the best physical fit.

While several of the brands featured within are still in business today, these advertisements are antiques, and should not be considered representative of the companies' current business, product or philosophy.

Medical knowledge has improved over the past century, but we'll still remind you that this book is for entertainment and historical educational purposes only.

Most image scans, photos and text were kindly provided by the United States Library of Congress and associated universities, The Internet Archive, Google Books, The New York Public Library, and private collectors.

If you enjoyed this book, please consider leaving a review on Amazon.com — and tell a friend!

Other vintage beer ads (including those for later eras), articles, photos and lots more good stuff from history can be found online at ClickAmericana.com.

*Beer, if drunk
in moderation,
softens the temper,
cheers the spirits,
and promotes health.*

- Thomas Jefferson

To be SOLD by
ISAAC HOWELL,

At his Brewery, in Sixth-street, near Arch-street,
BOTTLED BEER;
Likewise the different kinds of Malt Liquor, fit for immediate
Use or Exportation.
N. B. To be LETT, near the said Brew-house, a new Brick
Tenement, with three Rooms on a Floor. For further Par-
ticulars, enquire of   ¶   ISAAC HOWELL.

PENNSYLVANIA GAZETTE, MARCH 19, 1767

MOORE AND SNOWDON,
AT THE UNION BREWERY,
The Corner of RACE and FOURTH STREETS,

BEG leave to acquaint the Public, and particularly
those who are curious in Malt Liquors, that they
have prepared from the choicest materials, and now
ready for use, a large quantity of best pale Bottled Beer,
which they will deliver any where in the city, at the rate
of 6 s. per dozen, exclusive of bottles. Merchants, Captains of vessels, and others, who shall be pleased to favour
them with their orders, may be supplied on the shortest
notice, with any quantity, carefully packed and wired
for exportation.

THE PENNSYLVANIA PACKET, MAY 11, 1772

∫ The long S – which looks like a lowercase F to most
of us today – was commonly used in typography of
this period. It's also used in these ads as the symbol for
"shilling," the British unit of currency in use at the time.

WILLIAM INNES,

RETURNS grateful thanks to his good Customers,
acquaints them and the Public, he has on hand,
Strong Beer of the first quality at 45s. by the barrel or
half barrel; the same Beer bottled, by the groce or
dozen, at the lowest price; likewise, a light fine Ale
at 30s. per barrel in casks, or bottled at 6s per dozen.
Said INNES intends brewing Table Beer through
the summer at 15s. per barrel, and will send it out in
barrels, half barrels, or 10 gallon kegs. Owners and
Captains of ships may be supplied in the harbour with
fresh Beer when called for. Orders from the country
by land or water will be punctually answered.
Said Innes lives by South street, between Front and
Second streets.   Philadelphia, May 6.

PENNSYLVANIA PACKET, MAY 18, 1785

The New Brewery,

At the Corner of Dock and Pear streets, is now com-
pleated, and the different Qualities of
MALT LIQUOR
In readiness to be delivered to those who please to encourage it.   LUKE W MORRIS & CO.
Philadelphia, January 20.

PENNSYLVANIA PACKET, APRIL 19, 1790

8

STAFFORD, Nov. 22, 1769.
To be SOLD, at the BREWERY at
Marlborough, in Stafford county,

A LARGE quantity of extreme good
BEER and ALE, at 16d. and 11d. per gal-
lon, including the cask; the casks are good, and contain
from 40 to 50 gallons.
Capt. Thomas Casson will carry about 120 casks up
Rappahannock river, within 20 days from this time.
He will call at all the towns and Gentlemens houses on
the river, and will lodge any quantity for Gentlemen in
the forest where they shall please to direct.
Mr. Wayles, the brewer, has brewed four crops, and
has always made good liquor, and he thinks the present
crop will be better than usual, as the grain is very good.
He is so confident of his success, that he has agreed to
pay for all that is not good; and as a careful person will
accompany the Captain, who is a very honest man, there
can be no danger of adulteration in the passage.
The whole has been brewed since the 20th of October
last, and the beer will be fit for use in a fortnight, and
the ale in three days after landing.—Those who drank
of the last crop, prefer it to any they ever drank.

RIND'S VIRGINIA GAZETTE, DECEMBER 7, 1769

BOTTLED BEER,
By the Groce or Dozen,

FOR SALE at ROBERTS and GAR-
RIGUES BREWERY, in Fifth street near
the corner of Market-street.

PENNSYLVANIA PACKET, MAY 16, 1780

James Gregson,

At his BREWERY in Fourth-street, the corner
of Race street, serves private families and public houses with
PALE ALE and TABLE BEER, on the
shortest notice, by a line or verbal message.
Merchants and captains of ships may be served
with BEER and PORTER, in casks or bottles,
for exportation or home consumption.
•,• A good price for beer bottles. eptf.

PENNSYLVANIA PACKET, JUNE 01, 1784

James Newport

Informs his Friends and the Public, that he has for
SALE,
At his Brewery and Distillery,

In Front street, six doors above Arch street,
STRONG, Middling and Table Beers, of the best
quality, furnished at the shortest notice.
Also, prime Beer and Ale, for bottling, his own
make.
He has, as usual, Aniseed Water and other Cor-
dials, with a general assortment of Spiritous Liquors
Good encouragement is given to town and country
Store-keepers.
††† Constantly to be had, prime Rum and Wine
Colouring.   Dec. 7 2awtf

PENNSYLVANIA PACKET, DECEMBER 24, 1787

GREENWICH STREET BREWERY. JOHN NOBLE & Co. acquaint the public that their Bottled Porter is now ready for immediate use. The orders already received and those which in future they may be favored with, shall be executed with all possible dispatch. For the convenience of those families who reside in the east part of the city, a book is kept at the bar of the Tontine Coffee-house for the reception of their names, which will be sent for twice a day.

Captains of vessels sailing from this port, will find the above article worthy their attention. Particular care shall be paid to its being put up in such a manner as to become ripe in rotation, which will not only render it better, but prevent breakage.

All possible attention shall be paid to orders from any part of the continent.

Nothing shall be added in recommendation of this porter; it might with justice be supposed to call in question the judgment and good taste of their customers—for, after all, it is *their* opinion that must decide upon its real value: but, from the favorable reception it has met with, particularly to the southward, they are led to flatter themselves, that it will not only receive the approbation, but the solid patronage, of the public.

Orders from any part of the city shall, at all times, be readily and punctually complied with.

AMERICAN BROWN STOUT.—The subscriber has on hand, and is constantly receiving, a very superior quality of American Malt Liquor, similar in quality to the English, which is brewed expressly for his own bottling, put up in quart and pint bottles, for home use or exportation. Also on hand, Pale Ale and Newark Cider, ditto, ditto, of a very superior quality. Families residing in any part of the city, purchasing any of the above, will have it sent without an extra charge.
RICHARD WILLIAMSON,
s15 1w   19 Maiden lane.

EAGLE BREWERY,
61 Crosby street, first street East of Broadway, between Broome and Spring streets.

WRIGHT & DE PEYSTER, having rebuilt their brewery, and commenced brewing; have for sale, the different kinds of Ale, either in hogsheads, barrels or kegs.

Merchants, masters of vessels, and persons abroad, can be supplied, or have it shipped, as may be directed, and put on board free of expense.

From the extent of their present building, they are also enabled to send out table beer: Orders for which, for shipping ale, or ale for city use, will receive immediate attention, by being left at their brewery, or at 24 Broad street.

THE NEW BREWERY,
198 DUANE-STREET,

CONDUCTED by JOSEPH COPPINGER & Co will have ready for delivery in a few weeks, Porter, Pale Ale and Table-beer, of superior quality, transparency and flavour, brewed from whole grists of malt, with care and attention. Gentlemen, House Keepers and others who are particular in the quality of their malt liquors, will not be disappointed by applying as above. Those who may want Porter or Pale Ale for bottling or shipping off in cask, will find their account in dealing with this establishment.   Dec 11—3taw 1m *

New Brewery.
JAMES VASSAR,

RESPECTFULLY informs his friends and the public, that his New Brewery in the Village of Poughkeepsie is now finished, where his old customers and others may be supplied with Beer of different qualities. Also, good Yeast.

The great expence he has been at in building his Brew House, &c. makes it necessary for him to call on those indebted to make immediate settlement of their accounts.—Also, those who have beer casks belonging to him, to return them.

He has for sale a quantity of grains for cow and hog feed.

The highest price given for any quantity of BARLEY, at his Brewery.
January 4, 1802.   68

Brewery owner James Vassar (above) was the father of Matthew Vassar (below). Thanks to his very successful career as a brewer and merchant, Matthew became a philanthropist, and founded Vassar College in 1861.

FRESH ALE,
BEER & PORTER.

The subscribers having re-commenced *Brewing,* beg leave to inform the public, that they have now on hand a supply of the first quality of Malt Liquor, which they offer to their customers at the following prices.

PORTER,	$6 per bbl.	
DOUBLE ALE,	6 do	do.
SINGLE do.	4 do	do.
TABLE BEER,	2 25 cts.	per bbl.

N. B. Grains and Yeast to be had as usual at their Brewery.
M. VASSAR & Co.
Poughkeepsie, Sept. 27, 1820.   35—3w.

1800s

Pittsburgh Point Brewery.
THE public are respectfully informed that the Point Brewery is in operation. Porter fit for the Natchez and New-Orleans market can be furnished at any time at seven dollars ninety cents per barrel. Best Strong Beer for exportation or home consumption at six dollars and of a middling quality for families at three dollars fifty cents per barrel, delivered in whole or half barrels any where in the Borough, as usual. Orders from the Town or Country, directed to the subscriber, will be carefully attended to.

For J. O'Hara,
GEORGE SHIRAS.

November 3, 1806.

TOLEDO BREWERY

THE subcribers having taken this establishment, manufacture and have on hand and for sale at all times a supply of good beer, in barrels and half barrels. From the experience they have had in business, they feel warranted in saying that they can furnish as good an article as that made at Detroit or Cleveland. The Brewery is new and every thing in complete order, which is a guarantee to the public that they will not be disappointed or recieve an inferior article.

Orders from a distance will be promtly attended to, and persons up the river are assured that they can save transportation by purchasing here.

The highest price paid for Barley.

MERTZ & LEISER.

Nov. 14 1840.

1840s

TO PERSONS whose constitutions or state of health require a glass of Porter or Beer every day, the subscriber begs leave respectfully to announce that he has now bottled a large supply of PORTER, ALE AND CIDER, the qualities of which he warrants to be good.

To Invalids and Nurses Porter is recommended by the most eminent physicians as the best restorative and invigorator. In CHOLERA times it is admitted by all that there is no safer drink than Porter. Prices viz:

XX Brown Stout Porter 10s per doz. for quart bottles.

Single	"	8s	"	"
Scotch Ale	"	10s	"	"
Domestic Ale	"	8s	"	"
Cider	"	8s	"	"

Pint and Half Pint bottles lower in proportion.—Empty Bottles 6s per dozen extra till returned.

Po'keepsie, July 25, 1849.   91   M. SMITH.

PORTER, ALE AND CIDER.—The subscribers having made extensive arrangements for furnishing the above articles for exportation, would respectfully invite the attention of merchants and others desirous of shipping, to call and examine their stock.

The Ale and Porter have been brewed for us expressly for exportation, and will prove equal to the foreign in every particular.

The Cider is fined in a new and approved style, by which it can be transported to any part of the world without bursting the bottles.

Orders for the above in any quantity. furnished at the shortest notice, packed in a superior style.

MOFFAT & SWAN, No 6 Lewis wharf.

d6   is2m

CLAGETT & CO.,
PORTER, ALE, and BEER BREWERY,
EAST LOMBARD ST., BALTIMORE,
Keep constantly on hand PORTER, ALE an BEER, of the finest quality. Also, superior ALE and PORTER, in bottles. MALT and HOPS.
Orders promptly attended to.
FRESH YEAST every day.   tA20r*

LAGER BEER—From the celebrated Joint Stock Brewery in Philadelphia, always to be had by the Glass, Bottle, and Barrel, at HENRY WITTICH'S SHAKSPEARE HOUSE. North Gay street, No. 55, opposite Mr. Casparis' Apothecary Store.

This BEER is much used in Philadelphia and N. York, and has not only a very agreeable taste, but also the property of promoting the digestion. and of keeping the stomach in good order. It is a pure article, being mixed neither with drugs nor any other noxious substance. A l those who drink it will save the trouble and expense of taking medicine, Come and try it.   ma19 eo6t*.

METCALFE'S BREWERY.

THE subscribers are now making, and have on hand, a full supply of their superior CREAM BEER, and bottled ALE and PORTER; also on hand, 700 barrels of Ale, warranted to keep in any climate. Our manufacture is made from the best Kentucky barley. and cannot be beat. Let those who do not believe it order some.

METCALFE & GRAINGER,

dec3 d6   Main st., between Sixth and Seventh.

AGENCY.—The subscriber, at the request of several respectable citizens, and the solicitation of the Brewers, has consented to undertake the Agency of the celebrated PHILADELPHIA PALE ALE, brewed by Pepper, Smith & Seckel. The article being well known for several years by the citizens of Baltimore, as well as all over the United States, renders it unnecessary to give it a newspaper puff, it will tell for itself.

As I expect a lot of it in town in the course of this week, I would be thankful to such as would wish to give it a trial. to leave their orders with me at my BOTTLING ESTABLISHMENT, SOUTH GAY STREET, (between Baltimore and Second streets,) as early as convenient, so that it may be delivered to them from the wharf. The public's humble servant,

n7-sm&wtf   T. WALSH.

NOTICE.—NEW LAGER BEER BREWERY.—MILLER & CO. No. 245 North THIRD street, below Willow, would most respectfully inform the public that they are now prepared to furnish a superior article of this delicious Beer.

N. B.—This Beer is the same as the celebrated Beer of Bavaria.   d15-1w*

Cream and Amber Ale.

THE Subscriber respectfully informs the citizens of Wilmington, and public generally, that he has commenced the Manufacturing of Ale and Beer, on the corner of Orange and Front Streets.

JETHRO THAIN.

Dec. 14, 1947.   116-tf.

P. WILBACHER,
BOTTLER, AND WHOLESALE DEALER
IN
LAGER BEER, ALE, PORTER, &c.,
(Office on 18th, between Main and Cary sts.)
SPRING AND SUMMER SEASON.

Thankful for the liberal patronage and confidence in my establishment, from all parts of the Commonwealth and State at large, I take pleasure to state, that I shall sell during the Spring and Summer, my
BOTTLED LAGER BEER,
CREAM ALE,
and PORTER,
at the same prices as heretofore, viz:
Quarts. per dozen, $1 75 } 25 cts a doz allowed by
Pints, " " 1 00 } return of bottles.
Half pints, per doz, 50—extra charge for bottles.

Trusting, by prompt attention to orders, and offering always the best article, to share a still greater part of public favor, and give general satisfaction.

Goods for the country packed in barrels, and delivered to any Railroad Depot in Town, free of charge.

I am still Agent for the sale of Jacob Seeger's Baltimore LAGER BEER, and Dandelet's XX PALE ALE, the superiority of which is acknowledged by every judge, and I continue to recommend both articles for their pureness and beneficial effects to invalids.

☞ Orders left with Messrs. Duval & Norton, corner 10th and Main sts. Messrs Laidley & Robinson, corner 4th and Franklin, or at my store, will be promptly attended to. mh 18—dtJ1

RICHMOND DISPATCH (VA), MAY 5 1859

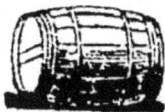

PHENIX BREWERY,
SANDUSKY CITY.

C. S. HIGGINS & CO. have just completed their new Brewery, No. 1. Water street; and having secured the services of an excellent Brewer from Pittsburgh, feel confident that they can at all times furnish city and country customers with as good an article of Beer, Ale and Porter as is manufactured west of Philadelphia. Families supplied with a choice article of Table Ale in quarter barrels.

Grains and Yeast always on hand and for sale cheap. C. S. HIGGINS & CO.
Sandusky, April 18, 1850. dtf

THE SANDUSKY REGISTER (OH), APRIL 25 1850

METCALFE'S BREWERY.

MY ALE thus far has kept good, and I can recommend the bottled to families and invalids; my Ale in barrels and half barrels is good but more suitable for taverns and groceries. I wish my fellow-citizens to call and taste for themselves. In a few days my Louisville XXXX Ale will be ready for use, a sample of which I shall exhibit at the Mechanic's Fair. I ask my brother brewers to send in their samples and compete for the premium.

All orders in my line thankfully received and promptly attended to.

Ale, Porter, Brown Stout, Hops, Corks and Bottles on hand and for sale for cash.
jy9 JOS. METCALFE.
N. B. A few kegs of prime Cider Vinegar for sale.

THE LOUISVILLE DAILY COURIER, SEPT 26 1855

LAGER BEER! LAGER BEER!—The Proprietor of the MILITARY HALL, No. 14 LIBRARY Street, invites his friends and customers, as well as the public in general, to try his Lager Beer, from the celebrated Brewery of Messrs. Dithmar & Butz, and he hopes they will be satisfied. Every Monday, Thursday and Saturday, Concert Music. je12-3m*203

PUBLIC LEDGER (PA), JULY 20 1850

St. Clair Lager Beer Brewery.

THE undersigned respectfully informs the public that he is now fully prepared to serve private families and the public generally, with his celebrated LAGER BEER, in bottles. All orders left at his Office, NO. 39 DIAMOND ALLEY, (near Wood street,) will be punctually attended to; and the Beer delivered to any part of the city or vicinity.
je28:tf F. G. SCHENCK.

PITTSBURGH DAILY POST (PA), JULY 29 1853

SOLE AGENT
FOR SMITH'S CELEBRATED
PITTSBURG XX AND KENNET'S ALE, AND
BOTTLED BROWN STOUT AND ALE,
F. VOLKINS,
Corner of Third and Jefferson,
jr13dtf Opposite Louisville Postoffice.

THE LOUISVILLE DAILY COURIER (MO), JULY 30 1856

1850s

New Beer Hall.
222 East Water St.
THE UNDERSIGNED takes pleasure to inform the citizens of Milwaukee that he has opened a new Beer Hall at No. 222 East Water street. He will always keep on hand the best of Beer, manufactured at his Brewery on the Watertown plank road.
FREDERICK MILLER,
Third door south from Spangenberg's Liquor Store.
apr24dtf

MILWAUKEE DAILY SENTINEL, JANUARY 1, 1857

This unassuming little ad was one of the earliest mentions of a small company that went on to become one of the biggest breweries in American history: Miller.

12

VAL. BLATZ'S PREMIUM EXPORT, MILWAUKEE LAGER BEER BY M. ULFFERS
PUBLISHED BY WITTEMANN BROS. LITHOGRAPHERS, JULY 1879

A brief history of
Anheuser-Busch & Budweiser

Logos in ads that appeared two days apart show when the company's name changed in 1879.
Adolphus Busch married to Eberhard Anheuser's daughter, Lily, in 1861.
He started out as a salesman, then purchased a large share of the company in 1869.

E. ANHEUSER & CO'S ST. LOUIS LAGER BEER
E. ANHEUSER CO'S BREWING ASSOCIATION
(ATCHISON DAILY PATRIOT, OCT 8 1879)

TRADE MARK ANHEUSER BUSCH BREWING ASSN.
ST. LOUIS, MO
(ATCHISON DAILY CHAMPION, OCT 10 1879)

According to Anheuser-Busch InBev, back in 1876, Adolphus Busch and his friend, Carl Conrad, created an American-style lager beer they named Budweiser. Conrad's company was the name on the bottle, and Anheuser-Busch Brewing was a primary investor.

While Budweiser was a huge success, Conrad's company failed in, 1883. As part of the bankruptcy settlement, Anheuser-Busch took over the Bud trademark, and they still brew that famous brand.

Below, see two newspaper ads and one brief news mention that illustrate how and when Budweiser changed hands.

C. CONRAD & CO'S
ORIGINAL
BUDWEISER
BEER.
BACH, MEESE & CO., Sole Agents,
₰15 TuThSu2p1m 321 MONTGOMERY ST.

C. Conrad & Co., manufacturers of Budweiser beer, St. Louis have failed. Liabilities slightly over half a million. The principal creditor is the Anhenser-Busch Brewing company, $94,000. It is believed the assets will be nearly half a milion. A meeting of creditors will be held next Monday.

Anheuser-Busch Brewing Associat'n
OF ST. LOUIS.
CELEBRATED BRANDS OF BOTTLED LAGER BEER,
"ANHEUSER"
—AND—
"BUDWEISER!"
☞ FOR SALE BY ALL DEALERS. ☜
A. F. EVANS & CO., San Francisco,
Sole Agents Pacific Coast. j23 tf3m3Tu

SAN FRANCISCO CHRONICLE,
SEPTEMBER 24 1878

THE HUMBOLDT UNION (CA),
JAN 20, 1883

THE RECORD UNION (CA), JUNE 23, 1883

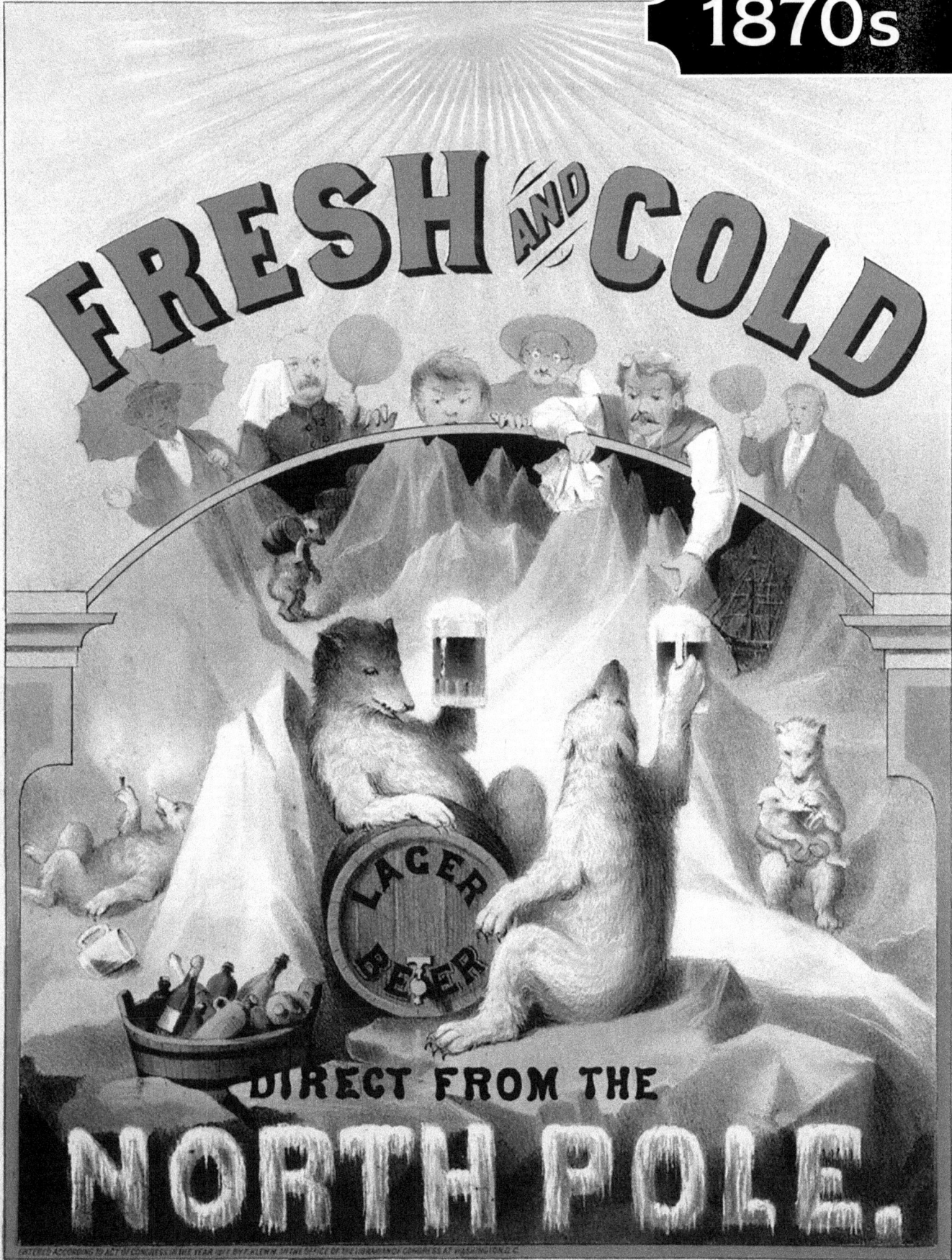

FRESH AND COLD - LAGER BEER DIRECT FROM THE NORTH POLE
BY A. HOEN & CO. BALTIMORE, MD | PUBLISHED BY F. KLEMM, BALTIMORE, C1877

LAGER BEER

H. & J. LAGER BEER AD BY DOMINICK I. DRUMMOND, LITHOGRAPHER / PUBLISHED BY A. TROCHSLER & CO, BOSTON.

AD FOR H. CLAUSEN & SON BREWERY, 47TH ST. & 2ND AV. NEW YORK | PUBLISHED BY WITTEMANN BROTHERS, C1879

FRANK JONES' BREWERY & MALT HOUSES.
PORTSMOUTH, N.H.
DEPOT 82 & 84 WASHINGTON ST. BOSTON.

FRANK JONES' BREWERY & MALT HOUSES, PORTSMOUTH N.H. (C1875)

LAGER BIER BY MENSING & STECHER, LITHOGRAPHERS, C1879

THE NEW YORK HERALD.

WHOLE NO. 14,725. NEW YORK, FRIDAY, DECEMBER 15, 1876.—TRIPLE SHEET. PRICE THREE CENTS.

DIRECTORY FOR ADVERTISERS.

SMITHS' NEW YORK PALE ALE

BREWERY, 240 WEST 18TH STREET, NEW YORK.

MEDAL AWARD AT PARIS, FRANCE, 1867.

ON AND AFTER FRIDAY, DECEMBER 15, 1876.

SMITHS' NEW YORK PALE ALE

WILL BE DELIVERED BY OUR OWN DRAYS ANY WHERE WITHIN A CIRCLE OF SEVEN MILES OF THE BREWERY, 240 WEST 18TH ST., NEW YORK

FOR SIX DOLLARS A BARREL

CASH ON DELIVERY.

ORDERS FROM THE COUNTRY ARE SOLICITED, AND UPON RECEIPT OF SIX DOLLARS AND FIFTY CENTS WE WILL SEND ONE BARREL OF OUR SMITHS' NEW YORK PALE ALE. WHEN THE EMPTY BARREL IS RETURNED TO BREWERY, 240 WEST 18TH ST., WE WILL REFUND, BY MAIL OR OTHERWISE, AS DIRECTED, A DISCOUNT OF FIFTY CENTS ON EACH AND EVERY BARREL RETURNED TO BREWERY, 240 WEST 18TH ST., NEW YORK, MAKING THE PRICE FOR CASH OF SMITHS' NEW YORK PALE ALE SIX DOLLARS A BARREL. ALL FREIGHTS ON THE EMPTY BARRELS RETURNED TO BREWERY WILL BE PAID BY US. ALL FREIGHTS ON ALE MUST BE PAID FOR BY THE PERSON RECEIVING THE ALE. SMITHS' NEW YORK PALE ALE, BREWERY 240 WEST 18TH ST., NEW YORK.

HAVING MADE VERY EXTENSIVE ALTERATIONS AND ADDED MANY IMPROVEMENTS TO OUR BREWERY, WE ARE ENABLED TO PLACE ON THE MARKET A VERY SUPERIOR ARTICLE AND AT VERY LOW FIGURES. OUR BRAND SMITHS' NEW YORK PALE ALE, MEDAL AWARDED AT PARIS, FRANCE, 1867. ON AND AFTER FRIDAY, DECEMBER 15, 1876, SMITHS' NEW YORK PALE ALE WILL BE DELIVERED ANYWHERE WITHIN A CIRCLE OF SEVEN MILES OF THE BREWERY, 240 WEST 18TH ST., NEW YORK, AT SIX DOLLARS AND FIFTY CENTS A BARREL, WITH A DISCOUNT FOR CASH OF FIFTY CENTS A BARREL ON EACH AND EVERY BARREL DELIVERED AND PAID FOR TO OUR OWN DRAYMEN ON DELIVERY:— MAKING SMITHS' NEW YORK PALE ALE SIX DOLLARS A BARREL, CASH ON DELIVERY. SMITHS' NEW YORK PALE ALE, BREWERY 240 WEST 18TH ST., NEW YORK.

SMITHS' NEW YORK PALE ALE

BREWERY, 240 WEST 18TH ST.

NEW YORK.

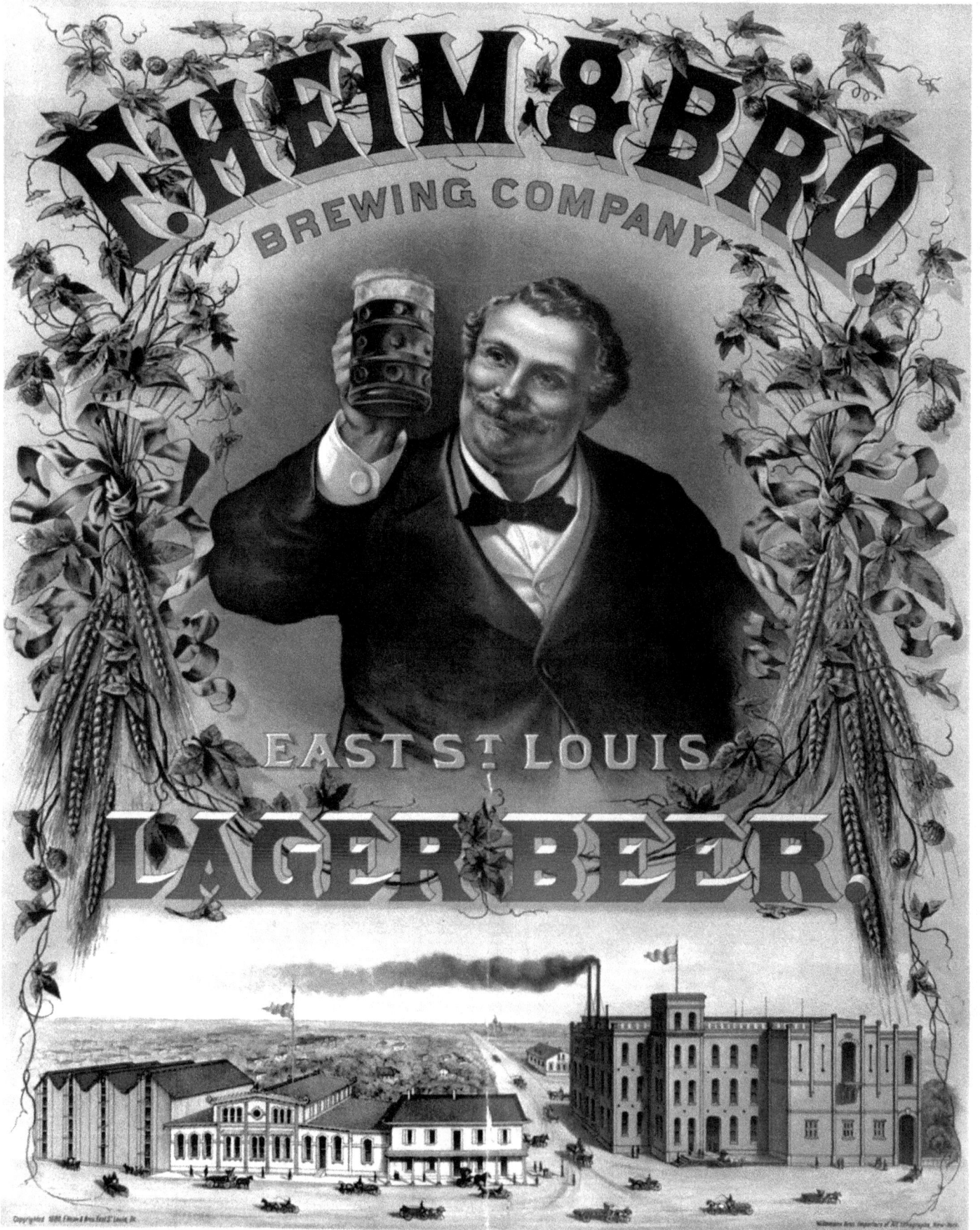

F. HEIM & BRO. BREWING COMPANY, LAGER BEER, EAST ST. LOUIS, MISSOURI | PUBLISHED BY WITTEMANN BROTHERS, C1880

BOCK BEER

PUBLISHED BY SCHILE, 14 & 16 DIVISION ST, NEW YORK - FEBRUARY, 1883

JOSEPH SCHLITZ BREWING COMPANY

HENRY UIHLEIN,
President.

ALFRED UIHLEIN, Sup!

AUG. UIHLEIN
Secretary.

MILWAUKEE.

FROM "BEER : ITS HISTORY AND ITS ECONOMIC VALUE AS A NATIONAL BEVERAGE" BY FW SALEM, 1880

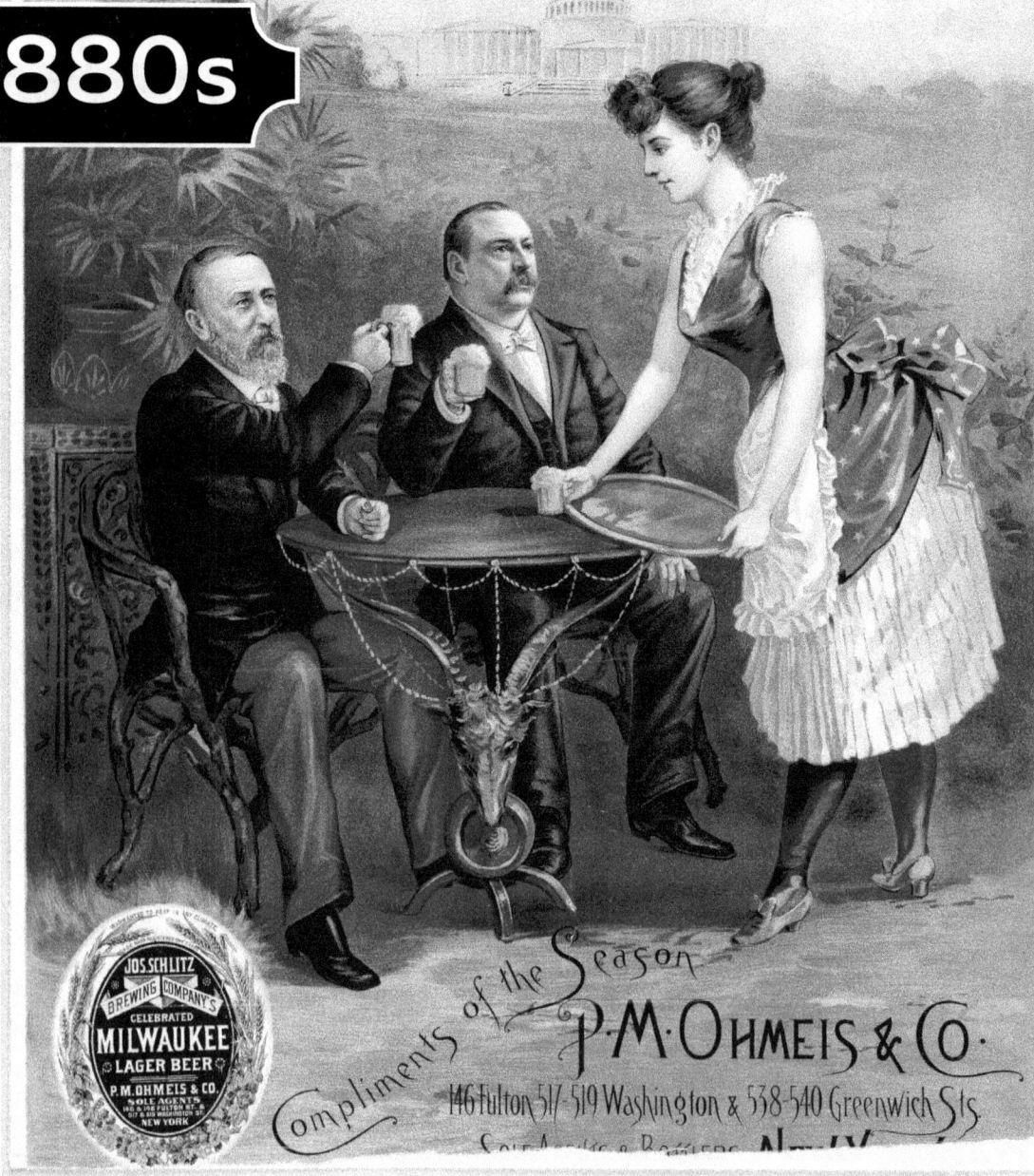

22   THE WHOLE NATION ENJOYS JOS SCHLITZ BREWING COS' MILWAUKEE LAGER BEER -, 1888

THE BREWER'S TRADE
LITHOGRAPH BY
HENDERSON-ACHERT-
KREBS LITHO. CO.,
CINCINNATI, OHIO
(1896)

1890s

ACTRESS
ANNIE REVERE,
WITH EDELWEISS BREW
(1898)

PERFECTION IN BREWING IS REACHED IN AMERICA

PABST MILWAUKEE

NEW AMSTERDAM

SOMETHING ABOUT BEER
Plain Unvarnished Facts of Interest to You.

A Western brewer in order to sell his beer in New York must sell it at a higher price. He cannot succeed in getting a higher price unless his beer is better. Milwaukee beer has been made famous by the **Pabst Brewing Co.,** and the universal recognition of the superior character of the Milwaukee product is due to their efforts to so improve the quality of beer, that they can sell it the world over in spite of local competition everywhere. A great many people know of this quality of the **"Pabst"** Milwaukee product, and ask for **Milwaukee** beer instead of saying **"Pabst"** beer or **"Pabst"** Milwaukee beer.

The law does not protect the name of a town, but it does protect the name of a brewer. The name of **"Pabst"** is protected. Because of this, if you ask for **"Pabst"** Milwaukee beer and notice that the trademark is on each bottle, you will be sure of getting not only **"Pabst"** beer but the very **best** Milwaukee beer. More than that it is absolutely pure and perfectly healthful. These last statements have a marked significance.

If you wish **"Pabst"** Milwaukee beer, **ask for it.** Insist that it shall be served to you. Many are tempted to serve a cheaper beer and reap a little additional profit. We invite you to pass judgment and are not afraid of your verdict, provided you get the real article, but before you either praise or condemn, be sure you are right. See that the label bears the trademark.
Ask for "PABST"

MILWAUKEE BEER IS FAMOUS PABST HAS MADE IT SO

BINNER CHICAGO

THE INVALID,

Those who lack vitality—the languid, those suffering from some accident which has made them almost hopeless of recovery, those with debilitating ailments, those with an uncountable weakness and lack of physical force, those with health impaired, or those slowly recovering from disease or fever, **are invalids.** No gift of modern science is to them a greater blessing than

PABST MALT EXTRACT, THE "BEST" TONIC.

It lifts, strengthens, builds is vivifying, life-giving, gives vim and bounce—it braces. It takes a subtle hold on disease, wrestles with it, eradicates it, fills the system with warm, pulsating blood, and gives the power to do and dare. For the invalid, therefore, be it father, mother, sister, brother, there is nothing to be compared with Pabst Malt Extract. The "Best" Tonic.

NEW-YORK TRIBUNE, JUNE 13, 1897

25

THE HOSTESS.

PROMO FOR ANHEUSER BUSCH BREWING CO, C1892

Conrad Seipp Brewing Co.

Lake Shore, Foot of 27th Street, Chicago.

Brewers and Bottlers
of the Celebrated..... **SALVATOR**

AND EXTRA PALE BEER.

Telephone South ————————— 8350.

West Side Nectar

WEST SIDE
BREWERY Co.
CHICAGO, U.S.A.

BREWED OF THE BEST MALT AND CHOICE IMPORTED HOPS

Sold in Kegs and Bottles,

Telephone West 129.   AUGUSTA & PAULINA ST'S.

McAvoy Brewing Company

AUSTIN J. DOYLE, President.

ADAM ORTSEIFEN, Vice Pres.   H. T. BELLAMY, Sec. and Treas.

Office, 2349 South Park Avenue.

Telephone South 8257.   --   Telephone South 8257.

THREE ADS ABOVE: CHICAGO EAGLE, DECEMBER 16, 1893

1896 CALENDAR, COMPLIMENTS OF JAMES EVERARD'S BREWERIES, NEW YORK, 1895

1890s

FEIGENSPAN'S BOCK BEER VIA THE THE NEW YORK PUBLIC LIBRARY

1890s

GEO. WINTER BREWING CO. BOCK BEER BREWERY, BY LITHOGRAPHER LOUIS KRAEMER N.Y. (C1900)

32

33

Wie Bier im Vaterland
gebraut ist—so ist

Culmbacher
hier gebraut.

Culmbacher is brewed by us like Beer brewed in
the Fatherland.

Culmbacher is a Tonic, a stimulant, a delightful
beverage. It's the most satisfying and the purest
dark beer brewed. 24 pts. for $1.25. Delivered in
unlettered wagons.

Washington Brewery Co.,
4th and F Sts. N.E. 'Phone E. 254.
oc23-th,s,tu-36

EVENING STAR (DC), OCT 23, 1902

The product of the

Aug.
Schell
BREWERY
is a
BEER

Clean and Pure

as it is manufactured in Glass Enameled Steel Tanks.

When you drink beer you certainly
want the purest and most wolesome
both of which qualifications are combined in Schell's.

Try a case at your home.
Telephone 8.   NEW ULM, MINN.

**NEW ULM REVIEW (MN)
AUGUST 27, 1902**

THERE IS NO OTHER JUST AS GOOD

1902

HONEST BEER

Since 1865 Hamm's
Beer has been hon-
estly brewed by the old German method—a purely natural
process.

Honest brewing has increased
its sale 500 per cent in five years
and the output is now 250,000
barrels yearly.

If you want a pure, wholesome beverage, order

**HAMM'S
BEER**

Supplied by Agents everywhere, or
THEO. HAMM BREWING CO.
St. Paul, Minn.

THREE ADS IN
BOTTOM LEFT
CORNER:
THE BEMIDJI
PIONEER (MN)
JAN 16, 1902

"HELLO THE BEER MAN"

"SEND MORE JUST LIKE THE LAST"

FITGER'S EXPORT BEER

Hello-o-o-oo!
MOOSE BRAND BEER

Are you acquainted with it?

It's a good friend —always dependable. Order a case.

DULUTH
BREWING CO.
DULUTH, MINN.

ABSOLUTELY PURE

Astoria Beer.

AN UNEQUALLED TONIC

**STRENGTHENING
INVIGORATING
APPETIZING**

BREWED FROM THE
FINEST QUALITY OF
BARLEY MALT
AND THE CHOICEST
HOPS
OBTAINABLE

SUPERIOR TO ANY
DOMESTIC AND EQUAL TO
ANY IMPORTED
— LAGER BEER —

BOTTLED BY
ATLANTA BREWING & ICE CO.
ATLANTA, GA.

PHONES 1249 - BELL OR STANDARD

36

THE ATLANTA CONSTITUTION, JUNE 6, 1902

1903

Budweiser's Greatest Triumph

Declared superior to the best Bohemian beers by the Imperial Experimental Station for the Brewing Industry at Prague, as announced by the following Associated Press cablegram:—

American Brewer Makes Best Beer in the World.

[Special to the Associated Press.]

Prague, Bohemia, Dec. 1. — The Imperial Scientific Commission investigating the different kinds of beer of the world has awarded the highest honor for superiority to an American product.

A correct translation of the results of their examinations is given below, with the Imperial and Royal Notarial and United States Consular verifications.

Upon subjecting a sample of BUDWEISER Beer, brewed by the Anheuser-Busch Brewing Ass'n, St. Louis, U. S. A. to a thorough examination, we declare it to be a fully matured lager beer. Its whole nature bears witness to the fact that only the very best materials were used, and that the greatest cleanliness prevailed in its manufacture. The product is not only similar to the highest grade of Bohemian Pale Beers in all its properties, but surpasses our best beers in keeping qualities, which is of the utmost importance.

Experimental Station for the Industry of Brewing, Prague, Bohemia.

JAROSLAV SULA; Supt. and Manager.

I hereby certify that Mr Jaroslav Sula is personally known to me as the Official Chemist of the Experimental Station for the Brewing Industry of Bohemia, and has this day executed and signed the above document in my presence. Prague, November the third, nineteen hundred and three. J. U. Dr. JOHANN SLAMENIK, Imperial and Royal Notary, Prague.

I certify that the foregoing authentication is under the official seal of J. U. Dr. Johann Slamenik, Imperial and Royal Notary, and is entitled to full faith and credit. In testimony whereof I, Arnold Weissberger, Vice and Deputy Consul of the United States of America, have hereunto subscribed my name and caused the seal of this consulate to be affixed. Done in this city of Prague this third day of November, 1903. ARNOLD WEISSBERGER, U. S. V. & D. Consul.

Budweiser

Is bottled only at its home, the

Anheuser=Busch Brewery

St. Louis, U. S. A.

JETTER'S GOLD TOP

BOTTLE BEER

Made by a master of the art of brewing—awarded highest honors at the American Brewing Academy —the only beer made from pure spring water— delicious—appetizing—healthful.

Delivered to any part of Omaha, Council Bluffs or South Omaha.

Order a case from the **JETTER BREWING CO.**

or HUGO F. BILZ, 1324 Douglas St., Omaha. Telephone 1542.
or LEE MICHELL, Wholesale Dealer, Council Bluffs. Telephone 80.

TOP:
THE SAN FRANCISCO CALL, DECEMBER 15, 1903

BOTTOM:
OMAHA DAILY BEE OCTOBER 04, 1903

$400,000 A YEAR GOING OUT OF EL PASO

1904

DRINK GOLDEN PRIDE BEER

MADE IN EL PASO.   KEEP THAT MONEY AT HOME.

The above cut is a true representation of El Paso's New Brewery now in operation and running day and night.   This New Brewery has a capacity large enough to supply ALL EL PASO and every town within a radius of 200 miles.   It is up-to-date in every respect, a model of beauty and a credit to, not only El Paso, but all the southwest. $400,000 a year is sent out of El Paso for beer.   Why not

Patronize a Home Industry and Keep that Money Here?

**Every laboring man, business man and professional man should insist on that money being kept in El Paso,
as that amount alone will employ many men, and will help to build up our city.**

GOLDEN PRIDE, THE EL PASO STANDARD LAGER BEER, is pronounced by the best judges to be the best beer in the market.   It is pure beer, fresh from the Brewery, not shipped thousands of miles.   You will find GOLDEN PRIDE on draught at the following places, call for it, note the fine flavor, note the big glasses:

Southern Club, the Trust Saloon, the Model Bar, the Atlas, the Acme, the Wigwam, the Gem, the Lobby, the Ophir, the Idea, the White Elephant, the Elias Place on the County Road, at the El Paso Brewery Park, Thompson's Place, St. Vrain and Missouri Streets.

EL PASO BREWERY ASSOCIATION

43

A Perfect Beer

Will loose all its pure, healthful qualities if it is not properly handled in the Bottle shop with surroundings absolutely clean.

Stegmaiers' Beer

is bottled with strict adherence to hygenic surroundings—the filling is done by machines (not hose)—every bottle is pasteurized after it is filled and sealed —this method is expensive —but our beer costs you no more than common Beer—try it— now. Phones.

STEGMAIER BREWING CO.

WILKES BARRE TIMES LEADER THE EVENING NEWS, AUGUST 21, 1905

Awake Ye Folks!

You who know the art of living, you know the time has come to drink Old Bull Stout. Cheer up!

When you've done a good day's work, a glass of good stout goes straight to the cockles of your heart. Old Bull is the stout made of the choicest selected malt and best Bohemian hops, straight goods from barley to bottles. Water from our own artesian well, 400 feet deep.

Chemist says it's the purest in Blair county And my master watches every step of the game. His business is Brewing for Health. If you want to get stout, don't try it on any stout but mine.

Old Bull

Partner with

V. A. Oswald, American Brewery, Altoona, Pa.

Look for this

Dog-on Good Stout

ALTOONA MIRROR (PENNSYLVANIA), NOVEMBER 15, 1905

1905

Children Are Not Always Good

IN THAT THEY DIFFER FROM PILSNER BEER MADE BY THE CITY BREWERY. IT IS ALWAYS GOOD AND ALWAYS THE SAME.

PILSNER

IS TRUE AND STEADFAST AND OFFERS THE BEST OF BEVERAGES FOR HEALTH, WHILE FOR FLAVOR AND TASTE IT CANNOT BE SURPASSED. PILSNER IS MADE BY

THE CITY BREWERY

SCHULTZ & STRICKER, PROPRIETORS.

EAST OREGONIAN E.O, FEBRUARY 10, 1905

SOLID COMFORT

Before retiring when a man can smoke his cigar and drink a glass of pure Beer to soothe his nerves. There is nothing like a bottle of Mayflower Beer for sound sleep, and for a general tonic and healthful beverage.

HAVRE BREWING CO.

Telephone No. 42, HAVRE, MONT.

THE HAVRE HERALD, AUGUST 11, 1905

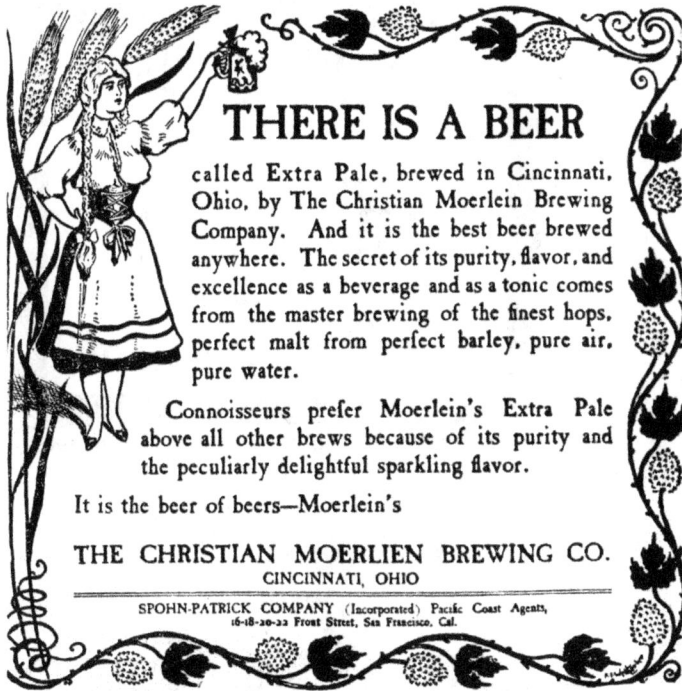

Gerst BEER

You cannot buy a beer which has been more expensively prepared than Gerst Dove Brand, yet it is sold as cheap as any. We carry cleanliness and purity to extremes, using the finest materials.

"*Gerst Beer, made famous by the sunny South.*"

William Gerst Brewing Co.
Nashville, Tenn.

PETER BELL, DISTRIBUTOR, PENSACOLA, FLORIDA.

THE PENSACOLA JOURNAL, AUGUST 20, 1905

Minnehaha

Represents a beer that is pure and healthful. It is the best beer brewed. Delivered to all parts of the city.

GLUEK BREWING COMPANY

20th Ave. and Marshall St. N. E.   Both Phones.

THE MINNEAPOLIS JOURNAL, FEB 10, 1905

...Louisiana Pilsener...

THE BEST BOTTLED

BEER

For sale at all first-class Saloons...

New Orleans Brewing Co.
BREWERS AND BOTTLERS

THE DAILY SIGNAL, SEPTEMBER 30, 1905

BREAD, BUTTER, BEER

A MINNESOTA MEAL AND A HEALTHY ONE

FOR THE BEST BEER BREWED GET

GLUEK'S PILSENER

"A BEER FOR THE HOME"

GLUEK BREWING CO. · MINNEAPOLIS

THE MINNEAPOLIS JOURNAL, SEPTEMBER 26, 1905

THE PEER OF BEERS
THE BEER OF PEERS

TRADE MARK

BULL FROG BEER

UNITED BREWERIES COMPANY, CHICAGO

BREWED AT

Northwestern Brewery
Phone North 2100

Monarch Brewery
Phone Canal 1252

SOLD ONLY IN BOTTLES

THERE IS ONLY ONE **BULL FROG BEER**

CHICAGO EAGLE, AUGUST 19, 1905

Globe Brewery BEER

A DELICIOUS FAMILY BEVERAGE

Won't you believe with us that pure beer is entitled to just as important a place on the home table as bread and butter? We honestly think so and frankly, would like to have you of the same opinion.

The careful and special brewing of **Globe Brewery Beer** is doing much to popularize the moderate use of pure beer as a beverage.

The very chasteness and clarity of this beer bespeaks the purity of its composition and the selection of choicest materials used in its brewing.

Its delicious cooling taste betokens the absolutely beneficial effect it has on the organs of digestion.

Get pure beer for home and table use—get **Globe Brewery Beer**. It is always pure.

When you order a case sent home, ask your dealer for the brewery bottling.

Hygienically brewed by

The Independent Brewing Co. of Pittsburgh.

Brewers of the far-famed Duquesne Silver Top Beer

THE DAILY REPUBLICAN, OCT 23, 1905

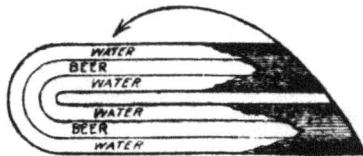

47

Proved Healthfulness

Scientists Affirm the Healthfulness of Good Beer

Purity means an absence of foreign matter —nothing else.

Cleanliness is a well known brewing ESSENTIAL. It is a matter of self-preservation with ALL brewers.

Purity and cleanliness alone do not assure Good Beer nor Healthful Beer.

Healthfulness depends solely upon QUALITY, and quality depends solely upon the ingredients used and upon the method of brewing.

Beer may be brewed from almost any cereal.

Many brewers use Corn as a substitute for Barley-Malt, because Corn costs less.

But the element of QUALITY, the essential of Healthfulness, must be lacking in such Beer.

Choice Barley, Selected Hops and extra quality Yeast are the prime essentials of Good and Healthful Beer.

This is a well known scientific fact.

We use the choicest Barley and Saazer Hops in brewing our Beers, adding a small quantity of Rice in pale beer.

These Saazer Hops, from a small province in Bohemia, have been found by Scientists to contain a superior quality of that wonderful health-giving substance—Lupulin.

Lupulin is creating a stir in the scientific and medical world because of its marvelous results in the treatment of nervous and digestive disorders.

We import a greater quantity of these expensive Saazer Hops than all other brewers combined.

Our storing capacity — 600,000 barrels, more than double that of any other Brewery in the United States — makes it possible for us to store (lager) our Beer from four to five months, the time necessary to thoroughly age it.

This perfect maturing brings out, to the utmost, the health-giving qualities of the choice ingredients used.

These are the facts relative to what constitutes good beer.

They are worthy the attention of every person who demands the best when eating or drinking.

Anheuser-Busch Brewing Ass'n
St. Louis U. S. A.
Largest Brewers in the World

CHAS H. MAYHEW, Manager,
Anheuser-Busch Branch,
Washington.

EVENING STAR (DC), AUGUST 03, 1906

50

At any time or Place

Luxus

REGISTERED U.S. PAT. OFF

The BEER you Like

No matter with whom you are or where you are—at lunch, at dinner, at home or at the restaurant, you and your friends will always enjoy Luxus Beer. It is always the same—always pure, pale, delicious and wholesome. It will never disappoint you in your entertaining. You will enjoy seeing others enjoy it and hearing them praise it. All who know good beer when they taste it know that they never tasted any other so good as Luxus.

And the beauty about Luxus is, it is just as good as it tastes and looks. Absolutely pure, made from the choicest Bohemian hops, malt from the best barley grown, and selected India rice, *and made right*. Then fully aged. It is the embodiment of perfection of the Master Brewer's Highest Art. That's why everybody likes it best of all. Why we say "The Beer You Like."

If you have not tried Luxus Beer, don't wait longer without doing so. If your dealer can not supply you, send your order direct to us and we will see that you are supplied promptly.

FRED KRUG BREWING COMPANY
OMAHA, NEB.

TRUTH (NEBRASKA), OCTOBER 13, 1906

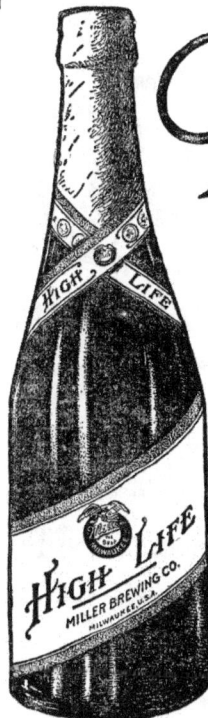

Miller HIGH LIFE
The Champagne of Bottle BEER

Miller "High-Life" Beer has that **rich, pure** and **pleasing taste** called the "MILLER TASTE" gained by perfection in brewing.

Cleanliness and **Purity** are our strong points and are very essential in beer making. We spend large sums annually in this direction, our experience being of **sixty years' standing.**

Our Malt and Hops are the very best money can buy and the **best obtainable** on the world's markets and are selected by **expert brew-masters.**

We **filter** all our beer and **sterilize** every bottle before it leaves our brewery.

The reason Miller Beer is so much better than other beer is in the way it's brewed.

MINNEAPOLIS BRANCH, 610 Fifteenth Ave. So.
N. W. Phone, Main 1149.   T. C. Phone, 1628.

MILWAUKEE

THE MINNEAPOLIS JOURNAL, AUGUST 30, 1906

1906

Would You be Strong ?

THEN DRINK LIMA BEER

That the regular use of Lima beer will give strength and vigor, is no idle claim. The "body" of Lima beer is barley malt, one of the most vitally nutritious foods, and hops, one of the best known tonics.

Lima beer nourishes the body, puts new vigor into the blood, aids in the digestion of other foods and tones up the entire system.

Get a case of this fine beer, drink it regularly and note the beneficial effects.

LIMA BREWING CO.
'Phone 37.

1906

THE HOME OF HIGH-CLASS BEER.

Golden Eagle Lager

—the most expensively brewed lager that money can buy—is produced in this modern brewery.

"Golden Eagle" COSTS DEALERS MORE than other lagers, but the QUALITY easily justifies the difference in price.

THE CONSUMER PAYS NO MORE for Golden Eagle Lager than for inferior brews.

On Draught ONLY at Leading Bars.   Call for It.

National Capital Brewing Company.

ABOVE: THE WASHINGTON POST, JANUARY 25, 1906
ABOVE LEFT: THE LIMA NEWS (OHIO) DECEMBER 3, 1906

GET IT OVER YOUR PHONE

WRITE, PHONE or SEND for a CASE of
PINNACLE BEER

For health and temperance, it is an unsurpassed home beverage, extremely heavy in malt extract, but containing only enough alcohol to aid digestion; not enough to intoxicate. Taken in moderation, no beverage in the world is as beneficial as Pinnacle Beer. The malt and hops are a tonic and nervine. The salts build up the bones, carbonic acid refreshes delightfully, and the pure mountain spring water quenches thirst, and carries away the waste from the system.

Try it for Health and Temperance

The NEW SOUTH BREWERY & ICE CO. (Inc.) Middlesborough, Ky.
Asheville Wine, Liquor & Soda Water Co., Asheville, N.C., Distributors.

THE RALEIGH TIMES (NORTH CAROLINA), NOVEMBER 1, 1906

54

Salt Lake City Brewing Company

O F ALL the many flourishing and prosperous institutions of which Salt Lake City and the State of Utah is justly proud, The Salt Lake City Brewing Company stands first and foremost among the manufacturing industries. The business of the company has been forging to the front by leaps and bounds and it has been nearly impossible for the company to keep up with its orders. Some of the chief reasons assigned for the rapid growth of this butiness, aside from the general prosperity of the country, are first: that the old time prejudices against beer are surely wearing away owing to the fact that the general public is gradually coming to know and realize the fact that

BEER CONTAINS LESS ALCOHOL THAN APPLE CIDER

All good beer, aside from containing only the finest malt and hops, must be carefully and scientifically brewed and properly fermented and aged, or it will not have that delicious flavor for which the product of this company is widely known. This brewery spares no necessary expense or labor to procure the finest barley, malt and hops that can be procured for the manufacture of their superior quality of beer.

The company does a very large business in bottled beer, and none of its beer is sent away to be bottled by amateurs in the country who lack facilities, but all is bottled fresh at the company's own bottling works, where the latest and best devices known are always used: hence, the goods are always artistically bottled and its "American Beauty" brand has met with such general favor that it is well nigh impossible to supply the demand for it.

In view of this inadequacy of the plant to meet the demands made upon it, the management, feeling so encouraged by its growing patronage, has decided to expend half a million dollars in enlarging the plant which is already the largest of its kind west of the Rocky Mountains.

The above illustrations, made from architects' drawings, show that no time has been lost in making preparations to meet the rush of next season's business. The contractors are now figuring on the erection of these extensive improvements, excavations for the foundations being already well under way. When completed, there is no other brewery in the United States that can boast of more complete appointments for the production of the excellent quality of beer for which this company is justly celebrated.

There is another point to which attention is called, which shows the consideration the company holds for its patrons, and that is that all beer is stored in steel, glass-lined, enameled tanks. There is not another brewery west of St. Louis that is equipped in this manner.

Mr. Matthew Cullen and Mr. Jacob Moritz are the owners of this great enterprise. Mr. Cullen is the President, and Mr. Moritz holds the offices of Vice President, Treasurer and General Manager, Mr. Philip E. McKinney being Secretary.

The Brewing Department is in charge of Mr. Oscar Lehmann, a graduate of the Brewers' Academy of Munich, Bavaria, in addition to which he has had many years' experience in some of the largest breweries in the United States. The extraordinary demand for their beer is the greatest testimonial possible of the expert knowledge of Mr. Lehmann. Fifteen years of service with the company has placed him high in the esteem of the Management, as well as the Public. This department is one of the utmost importance to the success of the brewery.

The capacity of The Salt Lake City Brewing Company, when completed, will be the largest of any west of St. Louis. All positions in connection with this enterprise are filled by the most capable men that money can procure.

The success of this Company is due more to the genius of Mr. Jacob Moritz than to any other cause. Mr. Moritz is ever on the lookout for improved machinery, in search of which he visits the trade centers of the United States, and it is never a question of cost, but always a question as to whether it will improve the purity and quality of the most excellent Beer that is placed on the market by this Company. His constant aim is to see that this Brewery is kept at the head of the list of like establishments in the country.

"This is the bottle, note it well

That has a story new to tell:

'I'm only a bit of glass you see

But I'm proud of what's inside of me—

Golden amber lager beer

Every glass brimful of cheer!' "

STANDARD BEER

"—the brew
for you—"

—a pure, wholesome lager beer,
a delightful and harmless family beverage
which, altho' it costs us much more to brew,
costs you no more than inferior beer.

ABOVE: THE SCRANTON TRUTH (PA),
SEPTEMBER 22, 1906

LEFT: THE WASHINGTON TIMES,
MAY 01, 1907

A New Departure

=Heurich's "Maerzen" and "Senate" Beers
=Are Now Bottled at the Brewery.

WE desire to announce that we have installed, at the brewery, A MODERN BOTTLING PLANT, which is conceded by experts to be the most complete and up to date of any in the country.

In the future the celebrated "MAERZEN" and "SENATE" Beers will be bottled under the immediate supervision of the brewery, thus insuring that these high-class beers will reach our patrons, at their homes, in the best possible condition at all times.

Finest materials alone do not make the finest beer. It is the combination of finest materials, perfect brewing, thorough aging, cleanliness, and proper bottling that produces the IDEAL BOTTLED BEER. All these requisite virtues are developed to an unusual degree in the production of "MAERZEN" and "SENATE." The results are beers justly celebrated for

Purity, Cleanliness, and Excellence

The label on the bottle guarantees the PURITY of "Maerzen" and "Senate," under the food and drugs act, June 30, 1906. See that you get the brewery bottling.

☞ Case of 2 doz., $1.75—50c rebate on return of bottles. Write or phone West 37. Delivered to homes in unlettered wagons, if desired.

Chr. Heurich Brewing Co.

25th, 26th, D and Water Streets Northwest

Pale *Perfecto* BEER

He likes it; you would like it. Ask for it at your club, cafe or restaurant.

WACKER & BIRK BREWING CO., CHICAGO

Ulmer Malt Beer is a dark, rich, nutritious brew.

CHICAGO EAGLE, JANUARY 06, 1906

59

THIRST

Is Nature's Warning

that the system needs moisture to withstand the enervating effect of the weather. Betz Beer is Nature's remedy—braces and nourishes—is food and drink. We deliver Betz Beer in cases of 12 or 24 pints free at your door. Call, mail or 'phone your order.

Jacob Betz Brewing & Malt. Co.

Telephone 348

A Light Beer for A Level Head

A light beer is just as essential as a moderate luncheon for a level head during business hours. Heavy, sticky, "bilious" beers are decidedly out of order during the business day—in fact they are out of place any time. A beer that requires digestion, instead of aiding digestion, is not the beer for you. The modern demand is for a light beer.

Luxus

The Beer You Like—Is The Lightest Beer Brewed.

It is as unique and different in this respect as it is in taste and quality. It is brewed especially to meet the refined American taste of today.

Luxus is "The Beer You Like"—it is what you have been looking for. It is beyond all argrument, the best beer brewed. Luxus is brewed entirely from the finest Bohemian hops, malt made from the world's best barley, choice, selected imported Indian rice, and pure water from our Artesian Springs.

Being a light beer, wholesome and appetizing, you can drink as much as you like of Luxus, with no after effect but a satisfied palate and a delicious sense of refreshment in the mind and body.

Test it today at luncheon.

Luxus is really different—it is not ordinary beer—Luxus is the most exqusite refinement of the brewers' art.

Brewed by the FRED KRUG BREWING CO.
OMAHA, NEB.
"EXPONENTS OF THE FINE ART OF BREWING"

Luxus

REG. U.S. PAT. OFF.

For Enjoyment
For Refreshment
For Health.....
The Beer You Like

Here Are Some Facts that every one who drinks beer will be interested in

When beer is made right, of the right ingredients, it is distinctly a *healthful* drink.

There is no question about that, because the highest medical authorities stand back of that statement. Your own physician will tell you the same thing.

Naturally, the beer that is made of the best quality of the right ingredients and brewed in the most scientific and hygienic manner, is bound to be the best beer.

Now, "LUXUS" *is* made of the right ingredients—that is, it is made of barley-malt with some rice added instead of being made with corn, or other cereal as some beers are.

Ask any responsible authority and he will tell you that barley is the right cereal for beer and that rice should be used in a pale, light beer to make it more wholesome and more easily digested.

Our malt is made from the finest barley grown and our rice we import from India—the best in the world.

The hops we use for "LUXUS" come from Bohemia and are selected expressly for us by our own expert. It is the superior quality of these hops—the lupulin they contain, that gives to "LUXUS" its unequalled value, as a digestant and general tonic.

As to the Purity of Luxus—it seems hardly necessary for us to urge the point. Of course

"LUXUS" is pure—the purity of beer is largely a matter of care and facilities in the brewery and there is not another plant in the world that can surpass ours in any particular except, perhaps as to size.

The Yeast used is an all important factor in the quality of the beer. A beer gets a great deal of its individuality and "character" from the yeast and there is not another brewery whose yeast can compare *distinctive characteristics* with ours. We guard it against all contaminating influences with infinite care because it might be called the very spirit of our brewery.

You might not realize the importance of all these details but each and every one of them has a direct bearing upon this beer of *quality*. It is all these little details combined into a perfect whole that—

Gives to "LUXUS" a flavor—a snap—a refreshing and permanent strengthening quality, that has never been equalled in beer making before. TRY IT AND SEE.

Have a case sent home today.

Let us know if you can't get it and we will see that you are supplied promptly.

Fred Krug Brewing Co.
Omaha, Nebraska
Exponents of the "Fine Art of Brewing"

LEVINSON'S

1209 SECOND AVENUE   **SEATTLE, WASHINGTON**

PHONES—Sunset Main 644—Independent 644

THE SEATTLE STAR (WASHINGTON), APRIL 24, 1907

OPPOSITE PAGE, CLOCKWISE FROM UPPER LEFT:

THE EVENING STATESMAN (WASHINGTON), OCTOBER 16, 1907
HOLBROOK ARGUS (ARIZONA), JULY 09, 1907
THE BIG STONE GAP POST (VIRGINIA), JULY 24, 1907
THE BIG STONE GAP POST (VIRGINIA), JULY 03, 1907

Anheuser-Busch

Reigns Supreme

The Growth in Sales is the Evidence

1865	. . . . .	8,000 Barrels
1870	. . . . .	18,000 Barrels
1880	. . . . .	131,000 Barrels
1890	. . . . .	702,000 Barrels
1900	. . . . .	939,768 Barrels
1901	. . . . .	1,006,495 Barrels
1902	. . . . .	1,109,315 Barrels
1903	. . . . .	1,201,762 Barrels
1904	. . . . .	1,365,711 Barrels
1905	. . . . .	1,403,788 Barrels

1906 - 1,543,468 Barrels of Beer

Budweiser

Sales for 1906

162,700,710 Bottles

This Exceeds that of All Other BOTTLED BEERS.
The high standard of quality, fine flavor and exquisite
taste have won for Budweiser its great popularity.

We court the
investigation of
all Pure Food
Commissions.

Anheuser-Busch Brewing Ass'n
St. Louis, U. S. A.

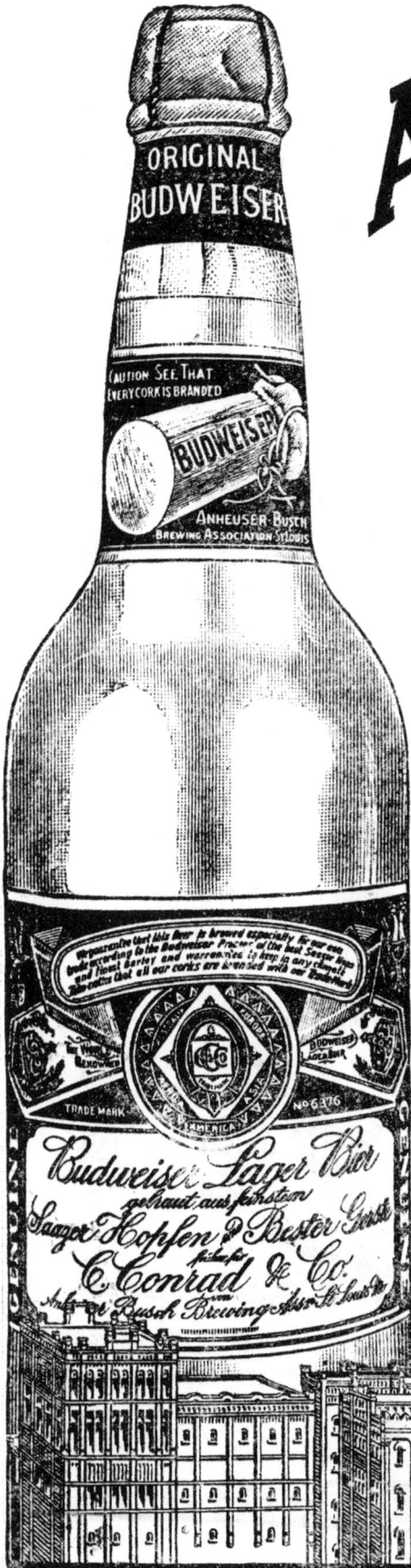

around the world

Wherever civilization has gone, Schlitz beer has followed.

It has been known in South Africa since the white man first went there. It is shipped in large quantities to the frigid wilds of Siberia. It is advertised in the quaint newspapers of China and Japan. Since Dewey captured the Philippines Schlitz goes there in solid train loads.

Schlitz has won against the competition of the whole world.

The reason is we go to extremes in cleanliness. Our materials are chosen from among the best grown by one of our partners. Our brewing is watched by another. The beer is cooled in filtered air. It is aged for months in glass lined steel tanks. Every bottle is sterilized. There are no impurities, no biliousness in Schlitz.

It keeps in any climate and always retains its delicious flavor.

*Ask for the Brewery Bottling.
Common Beer is sometimes substituted for Schlitz.
To avoid being imposed upon, see that the cork or
crown is branded Schlitz.*

Phone 3113
Schlitz Brewery Company
928 W. Broad St., Richmond

1908

Schlitz
**The Beer
That Made Milwaukee Famous**

The Lucky Key?

Beginning to-day, August 1st, you will receive a key with each and every box of one dozen quarts or two dozen pints of Wieland's Extra Pale or Brown Beer.

The Lucky Key unlocks a drawer within a handsome safe — it contains One Hundred Dollars.

If any one of the keys you receive with a box of John Wieland's Beer will unlock (that drawer) it's the Lucky Key —One Hundred Dollars is yours and the safe too!

Ask for Wieland's when ordering beer—get the Lucky Key, the safe and the one hundred dollars.

Write your name and address on the tags attached to keys—deposit your key or keys on or before noon, Monday, August 31st, 1908, at the store of Brown Bros. & Co., 664 Market Street, next to Chronicle (where the safe is now on exhibition), on which date the safe drawer will be opened.

If you have the Lucky Key, the money and safe will be sent to your address—or if you attend the opening and own the Lucky Key the money and safe is yours; you can dispose of it as you wish.

Keys returned later than the time and date stated will not be applied to the lock and will be discarded.

Drink Wieland's Beer

Every method known to the science and art of brewing has been employed to perfect Wieland's Beer.

Sparkling with life, snap and zest, Wieland's Beer is the key to health, invigorating—possessing quality resulting from the careful selection of hardy barley, perfect hops, combined with master brewers' skill to brew for discriminating tastes.

Perfect for the table—the ideal home beer.

Brewery's Own Bottling

Order a box of Wieland's Beer to-day—from your grocer. Costs you no more than other beers. **Get the Lucky Key!** You cannot buy a key—they are given free with your order.

JOHN WIELAND BREWERY
SAN FRANCISCO, CAL.

NOTICE.—Each month a safe containing one hundred dollars will be given away. It is important that you deposit your key or keys on time and at the place stated, as you may have the Lucky Key—the safe and money must go to its rightful owner. In the event of the Lucky Key not being returned, the safe and money will be given over to charity.

John Wieland's Extra Pale
John Wieland Brewery
SAN FRANCISCO, U.S.A.
BREWERY'S OWN BOTTLING

Name

COPYRIGHT 1908
BY
F. J. COOPER
ADVERTISING AGENCY
SAN FRANCISCO, CAL.

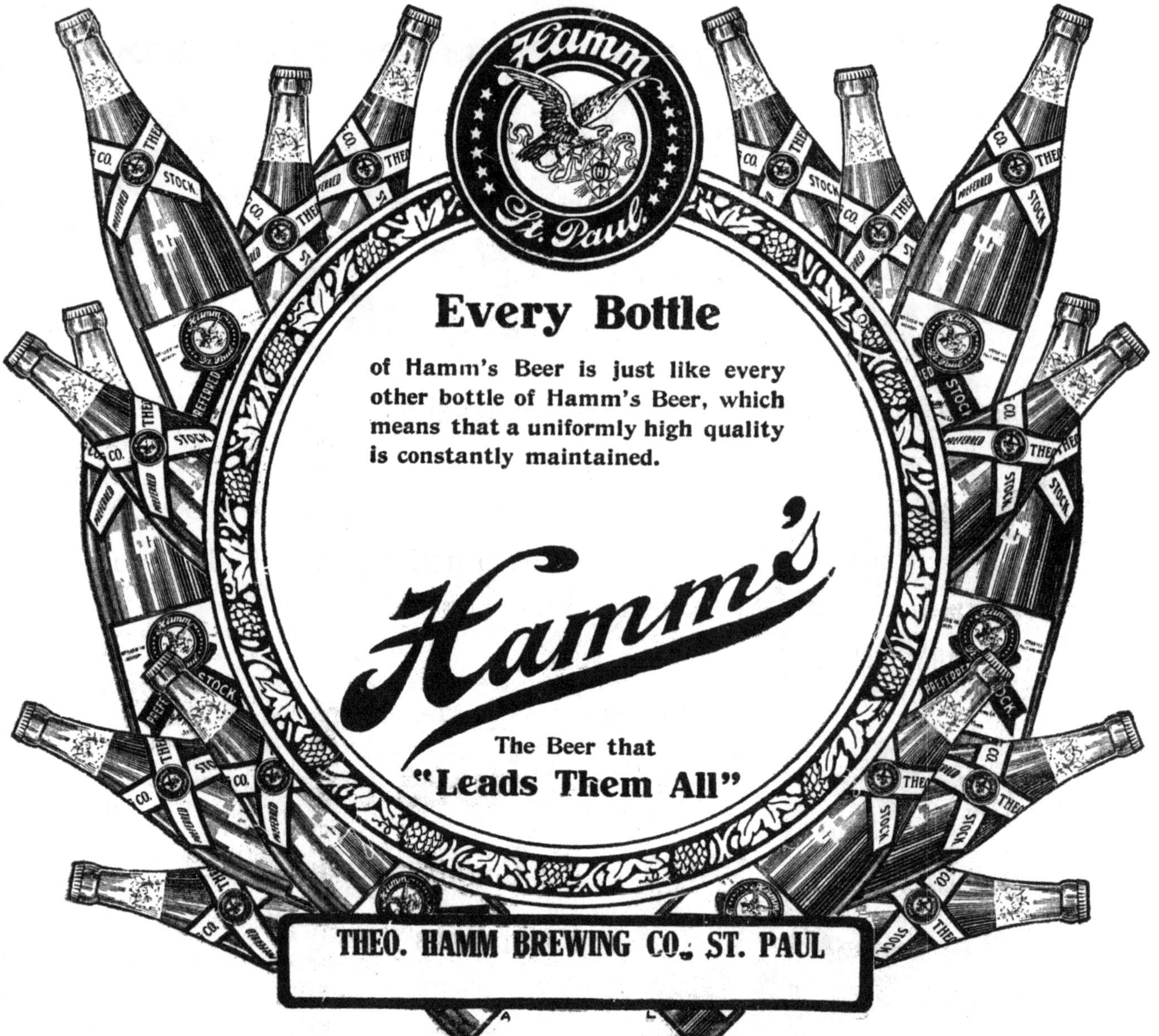

Hamm
St. Paul
Every Bottle
of Hamm's Beer is just like every other bottle of Hamm's Beer, which means that a uniformly high quality is constantly maintained.
Hamm's
The Beer that
"Leads Them All"
THEO. HAMM BREWING CO., ST. PAUL

YELLOWSTONE MONITOR (MONTANA), JULY 16, 1908

1908

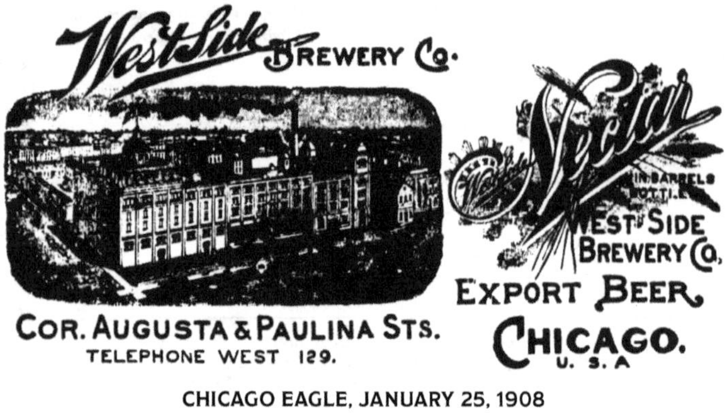

West Side Brewery Co.
Cor. Augusta & Paulina Sts.
Telephone West 129.
Nectar
In Barrels
West Side
Brewery Co.
Export Beer
Chicago.
U. S. A

CHICAGO EAGLE, JANUARY 25, 1908

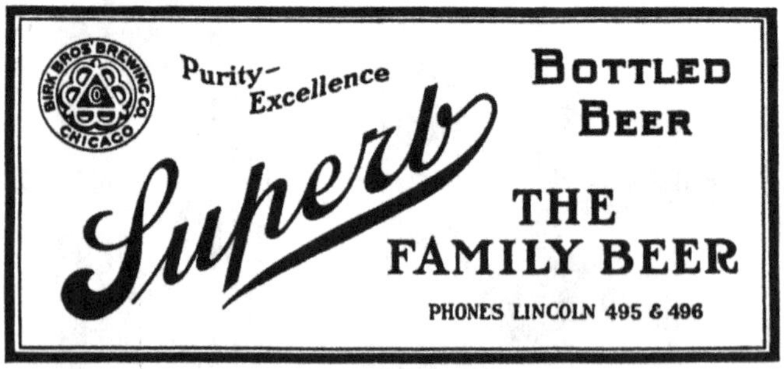

Birk Bros' Brewing Co.
Chicago
Purity-
Excellence
Superb
Bottled
Beer
THE
FAMILY BEER
PHONES LINCOLN 495 & 496

CHICAGO EAGLE, DECEMBER 19, 1908

Dortmunder
High Grade Beers
EXTRA PALE
DORTMUNDER DOPPEL
SALVATOR
BERGHOFF'S SELECT
GEO. A. BLETTNER
MANAGER CHICAGO BRANCH
Telephone South 570
2342-48 La Salle Street

CHICAGO EAGLE, DECEMBER 19, 1908

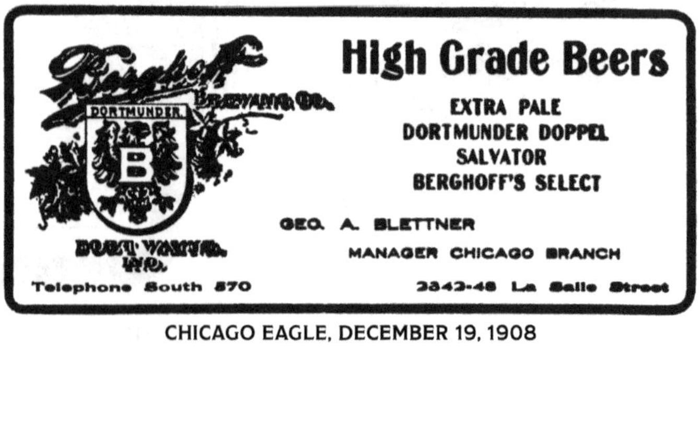

Iron City Brewery 1870

Prosperity-Progress

Since 1810 when the first brewery, now belonging to this company, was established, we have led in the development of the brewing industry of this city.
In fact it is no exaggeration to say that

The History of the Brewing Industry
in Pittsburgh
IS THE STORY OF
The Pittsburgh Brewing Company

Today we are operating some of the oldest established breweries in Allegheny County—breweries which have earned and continuously maintained a reputation for brewing good beer. These eight breweries

EBERHARDT & OBER BREWERY   STRAUB BREWERY
BAEUERLEIN BREWERY   IRON CITY BREWERY
WAINWRIGHT BREWERY   WINTER BREWERY
PHOENIX BREWERY   KEYSTONE BREWERY

are models of modern equipment, sanitary and hygienic excellence, ranking among the foremost of the great breweries of the Country.

PITTSBURGH BREWING COMPANY
BEER————————ALE————————PORTER

are made from the finest hops and malted barley by old and experienced brewers, who take pride in making this Company's product

ALWAYS THE BEST.

All good Cafes and Hotels serve P. B. Co. Beer, all good Dealers will send it to your home on receipt of phone order.

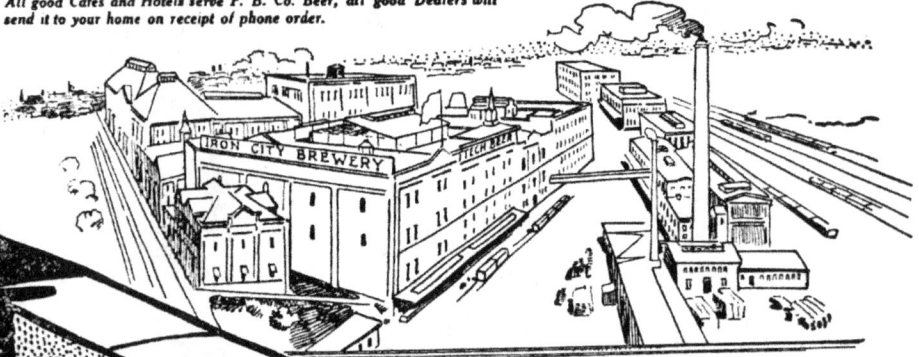

Iron City Brewery 1908

PITTSBURGH DAILY POST (PENNSYLVANIA), SEPTEMBER 30, 1908

Banquet Beer

The Beer of Purity and Flavor

Banquet Beer

is not only faultlessly brewed, with the purest water from the best selected barley and hops, but it is carefully and properly aged, giving that inimitable flavor.

Don't take our word for it. Try it and see for yourself.

Guaranteed under the Food and Drug Act of June 30th 1906. Serial No. 3742.

"Iowa Products for Iowa People"

Dubuque Brewing & Malting Co.
Dubuque, Iowa.

R. W. Yourex Co.
Wholesale Dealers

For twenty years

the beer of beers.

E. ROBINSON'S SONS'
PILSENER BEER
the brewery bottling

Pre-eminently the brew for the home, because of its unquestionable purity, rich food values and adequate age.

A dollar pays for the delivery of a case of two dozen pints to most any point in N. E. Pennsylvania. Old 'Phone, 470—New 'Phone, 542.

"San Diego"

'The Beer of Quality"--that's the name **"San Diego"** beer has been given by people who know good beer when they taste it.

"San Diego" beer is the product of the latest process of scientific beer-making ideas--and a trial will convince you that "San Diego" beer is second to none as a quality beer.

We would like to have you try a dozen bottles of "San Diego" beer---see for yourself why "San Diego" beer has jumped into favor so quickly.

Phone Main 157 and we'll be pleased to fill your orders promptly.

If you once try "San Diego" beer you'll never be satisfied with any other beer.

1908

CLOCKWISE FROM UPPER LEFT:

THE DES MOINES REGISTER (IOWA)
JANUARY 10, 1908

THE SCRANTON REPUBLICAN (PA)
SEPTEMBER 1, 1908

THE BAKERSFIELD CALIFORNIAN
JULY 15, 1908

1908

THE DRINK OF THE GREAT.

THE DRINK OF WARRIORS, STATESMEN—CENTURIES OF EXPERIENCE.

Drinking Citizens, Soldiers, and Sailors Have Conquered the World.

WORLD'S DECISIVE BATTLES WON BY BEER DRINKERS.

Beer Drinking Armies Smashed Napoleon at Waterloo.

THE GRAIN OF THE GODS.

BARLEY—THE NOBLEST OF THE CEREALS.

It Quickens With Life.

FOOD VALUE OF MALT BREWS.

SCIENTIFIC EVIDENCE.

Profound Study of Foods and Drinks—What an Eminent Member of Royal College of Surgeons Says.

THE TEMPERANCE VALUE OF BEER.

A REMARKABLE TRIBUTE.

What the Greatest of English Scientists Said.

Budweiser

ORIGINAL BUDWEISER

CAUTION SEE THAT EVERY CORK IS BRANDED

BUDWEISER
ANHEUSER-BUSCH
BREWING ASSOCIATION St. LOUIS

Six Thousand Men

are employed at the

Anheuser-Busch Plant

(THE HOME OF BUDWEISER)

Wholesome beer is their regular every-day drink, and nowhere in the world can be found finer specimens of healthy manhood.

They love their homes, they are good, honest citizens, temperate, patriotic and true.

750,000 such men are on the pay-rolls of America's breweries (and their allied industries) receiving good living wages; and—directly dependent upon their pay envelopes are not less than 4,000,000 women and children.

The Brewing Industry is now the sixth largest in America, and pays annually at least Two Hundred Millions of Dollars for farm products, and a like sum for manufactured articles. This year 6,448,000 acres were planted in *barley alone*, and 153,317,000 bushels harvested. Over 400,000 people engaged in farming are required to produce these crops.

Only the choicest materials are used for America's favorite beverage by the

World's Largest Brewery

Anheuser-Busch, St. Louis, U. S. A.

Budweiser Lager Bier
gebraut aus feinstem
Saazer Hopfen und Bester Gerste
früher für
C. Conrad & Co.
Anheuser-Busch Brewing Ass'n St. Louis Mo.

TRADE MARK

No. 6376

MASSACHUSETTS PASTOR BELIEVES IN LICENSE

HAS REFUSED TO JOIN ANTI-SALOON LEAGUE

Maine Experience Prompted Him to Fight Against Prohibition.

AN IRISH PATRIOT'S OPINION.

Henry Grattan, Whose Eloquence Stirred the Last Irish Parliament in College Green, Dublin.

73

GEORGE EHRET'S LAGER BEER

NEW YORK'S STANDARD AND FAVORITE

One Million Barrels Brewed Every Year

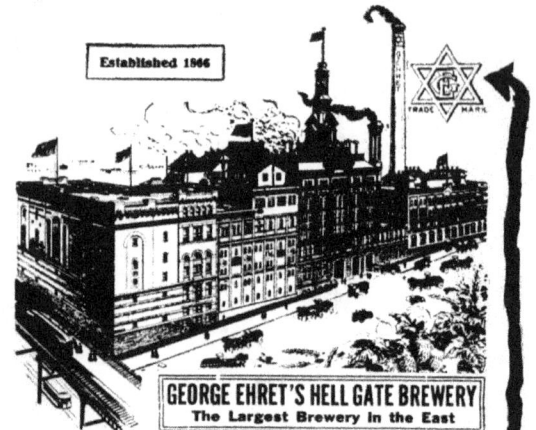

1909

THE SUN (NEW YORK, NY) SEPTEMBER 27, 1909

1909

CLOCKWISE FROM UPPER LEFT:

THE BROOKLYN DAILY EAGLE
SEPTEMBER 22, 1909

OMAHA DAILY BEE
AUGUST 29, 1909

THE SAN FRANCISCO CALL
APRIL 06, 1909

Christmas week is a time for social calls. Be ready—
have a case of FEIGENSPAN XXX AMBER ALE on hand.

ITS

POPULARITY

Made us the largest producers of
Ale in the United States.

Made necessary a larger bottling
department, the largest in New
Jersey, to meet the demands for
our Brewery Bottled Ale.

You can tell the genuine by the labels on the bottle and neck.
On draught where draught goods are sold.

Wholesale Dealer
and Distributor
'Phone 223.

JAMES B. SHANNON,
Commerce and Market Streets, Norwich.

ABOVE: THE MARION WEEKLY STAR (OHIO) APRIL 3, 1909

RIGHT: NEW YORK TRIBUNE APRIL 9, 1909

BELOW: OMAHA DAILY BEE (NEBRASKA) JUNE 20, 1909

NORWICH BULLETIN (CT), NOVEMBER 24, 1909

LOS ANGELES HERALD, AUGUST 07, 1909

The Value of Good Pure Beer

"In the New England colonies the lawmakers adopted a statute by which they granted immunity from taxes and an additional prize in money, to any brewer who should be sufficiently energetic to manufacture more than 500 barrels of 'honest beer' in a single year, for they held that beer was a beverage which not only added to the prosperity of the country by giving the farmer a profitable market for the grain he might be able to raise, but it supplied the people with a drink of such mild form that, instead of leading to intoxication, it actually contributed to the spread of that temperate spirit upon which the 'good order' of the colony so much depended."

Americana Encyclopedia.

Even in those early days the value of good, pure, wholesome beer was known. Think, then, of the value of the beer today which has the advantage of modern facilities and all that science has revealed to advance the art of brewing in the past century.

The man who drinks

Blue and Gold Lager

is taking a mild, stimulating beverage filled with nutrition in concentrated form.

Blue and Gold is the essence of barley malt and hops, two of nature's gifts to man that abound in nutritive and tonic qualities.

Order a case of Blue and Gold from your dealer and see what a real good beer tastes like.

BLUE AND GOLD BEER
Telephone Market 82

Blue and Gold Beer

1909

CLOCKWISE FROM UPPER LEFT:

TONOPAH DAILY BONANZA (NV) JULY 08, 1909

EVENING BULLETIN (HONOLULU, HI) SEPTEMBER 11, 1909

SAN FRANCISCO CHRONICLE (CA) APRIL 23, 1909

THE ALLENTOWN DEMOCRAT (PA) JULY 27, 1909

Preferred for the Home

ROYAL PILSEN
THE BEER
THAT
SATISFIES
ALL
TASTES

Why is

ROYAL PILSEN BEER

Preferred for the home and for the Club?

---Because it is a "LITTLE BIT BETTER THAN THE BEST BEER" made by others.

It is a satisfying and a beneficial beverage. The aroma of the hops and the fragrance of the barley make it an inviting drink at all times.

The barley used in making Royal Pilsen Beer is a valued food---the hops act as a tonic. Where there is need of more vitality Royal Pilsen Beer is the beverage to drink.

Royal Pilsen Beer is made in a great modern sanitary brewery. Through every step of its production the greatest care is exercised to promote its quality and to safe=guard against germs and impurities.

SERVE ROYAL PILSEN BEER TO YOUR INAUGURAL GUESTS.

Preferred for the Club

"That Delicious Beer" Bohemian

A Triumph In Modern Brewing

Buffalo Brewing Co.
SACRAMENTO

AMADOR LEDGER (CA)
DECEMBER 16, 1910

Health Boards Are Now Active

Seeking to ascertain the cause of fever's spread and check it. Their investigators always lead them to the deadly germ lurking in water and milk. There are no germs in the product of our brewery. Our beers are thoroughly pasteurized and pure, and the only real safe beverage now.

E. Robinson's Sons' PILSENER Beer

Affords all a substantial guarantee against the transmission of disease. It is germ-proof, leaves no distressing after-effects, keeps the head as clear as a bell, and is a most delicious and inviting beverage. It is bottled at the brewery under the most improved conditions. Order now. Case of 2 dozen pints is delivered for $1.00.

WILKES-BARRE AGENCY
15 WILLIAM STREET
Bell phone 1180.   New phone 1196.

WILKES BARRE TIMES LEADER (PA)
SEPTEMBER 8, 1910

Remember
The Hopsburger Man

Be sure that he is on hand to provide a cool, refreshing drink for the warm and weary hunter.

HOPSBURGER

The beer with "the taste that's a treat to the thirsty."

Bottled at the Brewery
Telephones: Market 278; Home M 1406

THE SAN FRANCISCO CALL, OCTOBER 10, 1910

When the Ducks Fly
The Hopsburger Man

should be represented in every gun club. His portrait on the label of a beer bottle is the sign of good fellowship and good beer

HOPSBURGER

appeals to San Franciscans because they are critical and want the best. HOPSBURGER is brewed in San Francisco and bottled at the brewery.

Ask Your Grocer   Order a Case Today

Telephones: Market 278; Home M 1406

THE SAN FRANCISCO CALL, SEPTEMBER 26, 1910

83

Omaha's Favorite

Absolute Purity, Scientific Process of Manufacture has made this

"The Beer of Quality"

M E T Z   **B R E W E R Y**

Metz Bros. Brewing Co.
Omaha, Neb.

OMAHA DAILY BEE (NEBRASKA), AUGUST 17, 1910

1910

NATIONAL BEER

—Now Bottled at the Brewery

If a Hard Worker—National will stimulate you to greater possibilities.

If Convalescing—National provides the needed up-building qualities.

If Banqueting—National completes the menu with utmost satisfaction.

FIRST LAGER BREWED IN SAN FRANCISCO

The Nursing Mother finds National the ideal food to sustain mother and child.

The Service at Home is improved through the health producing qualities of National.

The Social Glass is made more convivial by the deliciousness of National.

"The Best in the West"
AT ALL DEALERS'

National Brewing Co.
cor. Fulton and Webster Sts. San Francisco.

Office Phones—Pacific, Park 33; Home, N-3261 Bottling Dept.—Market 3111

THE SAN FRANCISCO CALL, OCTOBER 11, 1911

Same Price per Case as Other Beer

Here's a Beer That Is Beer

ORIGINAL HEIDELBERG
MORE THAN 7 MONTHS OLD

You Should Know This

That Germany is the original home of beer.

That in Germany the government has rigid inspection and condemns as unfit to drink, beer that has not remained in "lager" more than seven months.

That therefore German Beer is not injurious, does not cause sickening after effects, and tastes better than the usual run of American beer.

And Why?

Because the American brewers either have not storage facilities or do not care to lessen their profits (that long storage will do) in order to properly age the beer before bottling.

The Result

Most of the beer one drinks in this country is flat, bitter and causes "morning after" headaches—in fact, never is what it really should be—a pleasing beverage.

Original Heidelberg Is Aged Before Bottling

We have ample storage capacities and allow this beer to stand in the casks for more than seven months before bottling.

We use the best grade of Bohemian hops and malt, employ a German brew master, have every appliance that is necessary to produce a perfect product, and assure you a

Beer that is smooth, nourishing, pleasing to the taste and contains less than 4 per cent alcohol; in fact,

IT'S THE PERFECT BEER, and ONE TRIAL WILL PROVE THIS TO YOU.

Order a Case Today

TRIAL ORDER
A case will be sent C. O. D., and if found not as represented, money will be refunded and no charge made for beer consumed.

Phones: Ind. 2464; Main 2135

BELLINGHAM BAY BREWERY
Office, 2103 First Ave.

THE SEATTLE STAR, MARCH 01, 1911

The Most Popular Beer In N. Y. City Is Pabst Milwaukee

THE sales of Pabst famous Milwaukee Beer, Bohemian Brand (Light) and Doppel Brau (Dark) have been simply enormous since we announced four weeks ago that the families of New York could buy either or both at $1.25 per case of 24 bottles—the same price they had been paying for other beers not so good. Ask your dealer for

"The one best beer in the world"

PABST Milwaukee Beer

$1.25 Per Case

And insist upon getting it. If you don't get it, 'phone Bryant 24 and we will see that it is delivered to you promptly and at the regular price of $1.25 per case. Once you taste this best of all beers you will have no other in your house. Women like it better than others because it is sparkling with zest, yet not excessively bitter and because they <u>know</u> it is <u>clean</u>.

Sold by All Grocers and Wine and Liquor Dealers

ABOVE: THE EVENING WORLD
(NEW YORK)
OCTOBER 17, 1911

RIGHT: OMAHA DAILY BEE
(NEBRASKA)
SEPTEMBER 05, 1911

1911

A Beer Surprise!

Give yourself a beer surprise—taste some of this genuine old German lager beer—order a cold bottle of

Old Fashioned Lager Beer

—rich and mellow—delicious—satisfying. You'll be surprised how good it is!

Pint bottles only—of clear glass, so you can see it's pure and clean; the red or yellow wrapper keeps out all light, preserving the snap and life.

Order a case sent home—a splendid drink for all the family.

Douglas 1148. Ind., A-2148.

Save the Caps

from bottles of Old Fashioned Lager Beer and exchange them for valuable premiums. Ask us for free book of premiums.

Cackley Brothers, Distributors.

Wm. H. Bodemann, Gen. Sales Agent,
121 North Sixteenth Street.

MAIL ORDERS for "Old Fashioned Lager Beer" filled the day received. Shipped everywhere.

Now on tap

AFTER MONTHS OF CAREFUL AGE-ING AND SCIENTIFIC TESTING IN OUR NEW MAMOUTH CELLARS —

NARRAGANSETT BREWING CO'S NEW BREW ~

Real Pilsner Hops are imported direct from Bohemia for our new brew. During its ageing, "Gansett Pilsner" is sampled and tested in the good old-fashioned Pilsner way.

The quality of this beer is a high tribute to the skill and pains exercised by our brew master.

"Gansett" Pilsner

Has the Real Pilsner Taste Plus Narragansett Quality.

Those who like the distinctive flavor and snap of genuine Pilsner Beer, can now secure it under the name "Gansett Pilsner," with all the protection as to quality of ingredients, skill in brewing and care in ageing which the name "Narragansett" always implies.

Say "Gansett Pilsner" When You Order

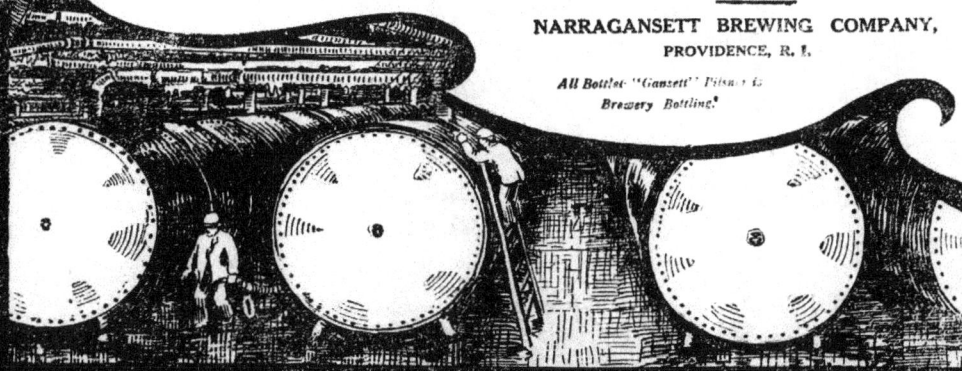

On Tap Wherever Narragansett is Sold.

NARRAGANSETT BREWING COMPANY,
PROVIDENCE, R. I.

All Bottled "Gansett" Pilsner is Brewery Bottling.

Our New Pilsner Cellar

We have built an entire cellar in which to store and age the new brew Gansett Pilsner Beer. This immense chamber is filled with steel glass lined tanks—the most modern and sanitary brewing storage vats.

There are three sizes with a capacity of from 300 to 500 bbls. each. The total capacity of the entire new cellar is 50,000 or more bbls. which can be stored here at one time.

The new brew, Gansett Pilsner has been ageing here in this cellar for many months in a low temperature.

It has been constantly tested by our brew master; and is now on tap wherever Narragansett is sold.

SAY "GANSETT" PILSNER WHEN YOU ORDER.

The Southern Trio

FAULTLESS LAGER BEER

Beers that are pure liquid foods

¶ The food value of Barley-malt and the tonic properties of Hops, as retained in good beer, are acknowledged to be beneficial to the human system.

¶ Observe, however, we said GOOD beer.

¶ Our Brewery is a model one, and our brewers are native Germans—men who learned their art under the world's masters in the Fatherland.

¶ We use only the best northern-grown barley and imported Bohemian Hops.

¶ These are the reasons why "Chattanooga Beers" are GOOD BEERS.

¶ Choice between our beers is simply a matter of taste as to "heaviness". MAGNOLIA IS LIGHT, IMPERIAL PILSENER IS MEDIUM AND ZACHERL BRAU IS DARK (HEAVY).

Order from our nearest agent or write us direct for prices.

"Sold wherever beer is sold"

THE CHATTANOOGA BREWING CO.
CHATTANOOGA, TENN.

Imperial Pilsener Style — Chattanooga Brewing Co., Chattanooga, Tenn.

Zacherl Brau

Magnolia — Chattanooga Brewing Co.

WILMINGTON MORNING STAR (NC), JANUARY 1, 1911

A Beer Of Quality

Our beer to-day stands as a peer among beers. It must be good, as we use only the best material in brewing that money can buy.

We have always strived to give the public a good beer, which accounts for the increasing output of our brewery. **SUSQUEHANNA BEER** is equal to any and superior to many.

TRY A CASE

Susquehanna Brewing Co.

Both 'Phones

THE WILKES BARRE RECORD (PA) AUGUST 19, 1911

NATIONAL BEER

NOW Bottled at the Brewery

The First Lager
Brewed in
San Francisco

YOUR GROCER
CAN SUPPLY YOU

Just 50 years ago the National Brewery was founded. National Beer was then the best, and, keeping pace with progress, it today meets every requirement of a most Wholesome, Palatable, Refreshing and Invigorating Beverage.

In our new bottling department every means and machinery of the most modern type are employed with a rigid regard for producing a Beer that the U. S. government does not hesitate to label "PURE."

PROPERLY AGED AND DELIVERED TO YOU FRESH IN DARK BOTTLES

Known by its zest as
"The Best in the West."

National Brewing Co.
cor. Fulton and Webster Sts. San Francisco.
Phones—Pacific, Park 33; Home S3261

Brewers of Pale and Dark
Lager (Muenchener style)

BECKERS

Becker's Best

PALE BEER BOHEMIAN STYLE

Purity--Quality--Tone--Flavor--

Better by test than all the rest--and made in your own state--Utah.

Conclusive reasons why you should order BECKER'S BEST next time you order a case sent out to the house--phone your local dealer or

Becker Brewing & Malting Co.

Ogden, Utah.

HOPSBURGER

A TEN STRIKE

SCORE

YOU CAN'T BEAT

The Hopsburger Man

You can't beat the beer that bears his portrait on the label of the bottle.

HOPSBURGER BEER

is a liquid food—a food drink—rich in all that is strength giving in the world's best barley—all that is nerve soothing in the world's best hops. Brewed under scientific and absolutely cleanly conditions by masters of the brewer's art.

Bottled at the Brewery

On Sale at All Grocers

Those Who Know

The Hopsburger Man

insist that his portrait shall appear on the label of every bottle of beer. It is a guarantee of satisfaction.

HOPSBURGER BEER

tastes good on all occasions. It belongs, by right of its clean, keen, snappy taste, to every out-door luncheon. Take it with you on your next outing. It will make the hit of the day.

Bottled at the brewery

On sale at all grocers

Market 278 - - - Telephones - - - Home M 1406

JACOB RUPPERT'S
Knickerbocker
The Beer That Satisfies

UNCLE SAM leads the nations of the earth in the production and consumption of lager beer and malt beverages. Father Knickerbocker leads the cities of America in both production and consumption. Uncle Sam has, for many years, received the annual wreath of victory for having produced the purest and most healthful beer beverages—a prize which, after a rigid investigation, he gladly places upon Ruppert's Knickerbocker Beer, *"the beer that satisfies,"* because there is not in the United States a better beer brewed.

THERE are several reasons why the Jacob Ruppert Brewery produces beer so good that there is none better at any price anywhere. We search the hop and barley markets of the world and buy the best; we use every precaution and adopt every sanitary method known to the trade in malting, brewing, bottling and delivering; we only employ skilled and experienced men in all our departments; every department is equipped with the best and most modern machinery ever invented for the making of beer; all our beer is bottled at the brewery and handled by us until it reaches the retail dealer, who delivers it in perfect condition to the consumer.

For sale by all dealers and on draught in hundreds of the best hotels and cafes throughout Greater New York.

[Our brewery is always open to visitors for inspection.

Jacob Ruppert, Brewer

Third Ave., 90th to 93d St.

1911

Beer and Coffee

—Their Opposite Effects

Caffeine, (or theine), the alkaloid principle of coffee, is a drug detrimental to the human system. Its evil effects are most noticeable to many persons after drinking a cup or two of coffee in the evening. They can't sleep.

Directly opposite to this is the effect of a glass or two of Oshkosh beer taken during the evening. It soothes and quiets the nerves, producing sweet, refreshing sleep

We are pushing Oshkosh beer as a substitute for coffee and would like to have you try it.

An order to us will bring you promptly a case of pints or quarts as you desire.

Oshkosh Brewing Co.

1631 Doty Street

Phone 188

HIGHLANDER

BOTTLE
BEER

Will Be on the Market From Now On

We Have Made Special Efforts on This Brew and Have Succeeded in Placing on the Market a Strictly High Grade Product

FAMILY TRADE SOLICITED

GARDEN CITY BREWING CO.

Bell 125——PHONES——Ind. 641

THE FAMOUS
CREAM OF MALT BEER
IS BREWED SOLELY BY THE

J. L. Hoerber Brewing Company

1617 to 1619 21st Place
Telephone Canal 138
CHICAGO

Prima Beer

GIVES SATISFACTION

BREWED BY
The Independent Brewing Assn
CHICAGO, ILL.

In the Heart of Homes

The beer for family use, above all others, should be bottled at the Brewery.

Do you know that the only sanitary way of bottling beer is at the Brewery, where the empty bottles can be thoroughly Sterilized and the filled bottles properly Pasteurized?

PETER DOELGER
FIRST PRIZE BOTTLED BEER
EXPRESSLY FOR THE HOME

is the Beer of Beers for the entire family, the Beer that is entitled to its place in the Heart of Homes.

It is bottled at the brewery exclusively. When the pure beer has been poured into a thoroughly Sterile bottle, automatically capped and sealed, the filled bottle is subjected to perfect Pasteurization, which will kill any and all germ life that may otherwise defy even the greatest precautions.

$1.25 the case of 24 bottles—one cent a bottle more than the ordinary beer.
A little higher in price—a great deal higher in quality.

Order a trial case from your regular dealer. If he does not carry it, kindly let us know, we will see that you are promptly supplied.

An Invitation

A personal inspection of our Model Brewery and Bottling Plant will prove to be an education well worth while.

Come any day, you will receive a most courteous welcome.

Peter Doelger

PETER DOELGER FIRST PRIZE BREWERY, Bottling Department, 407-433 East 55th Street, Telephone 2370 Plaza New York City

Beer Before the War of Independence

Over a century and a quarter before General George Washington, the Father of his Country, took command of the Armies of the Revolution, Father Knickerbocker, through his Dutch settlers built breweries and brewed beer in what was then known as New Netherland, at present New York. During the war for independence the brave sires and sons of liberty who fought to free the New World from the fetters of foreign bondage were supplied, while tenting on the old camp grounds, with beer brewed in old New York.

The Ruppert Brewery to-day stands as a model of perfection and is one of the greatest breweries in the world—the most modern institution of its kind in New York. Seeing is believing and we invite you to SEE how we make and handle our beers, especially in our bottling houses, where everything is handled with such perfect sanitation and scientific cleanliness.

JACOB RUPPERT'S
KNICKERBOCKER BEER
"THE BEER THAT SATISFIES"

Our bottled beers supplied to families by Retail Dealers.　　On draught at best hotels, restaurants and cafes.

The Sunshine of lager beer satisfaction radiates from every bottle of Ruppert's Knickerbocker. Every glass is a sparkling draught of exquisite taste and is as pure as any Brewer's skill can possibly create. Our entire establishment is equipped with the very latest mechanical inventions and sanitary devices known to the art of brewing. Nearly everybody is drinking

JACOB RUPPERT'S
Knickerbocker
The Beer That Satisfies

Our sanitary methods of sterilizing the bottles before they are filled, and the scientific process of pasteurizing the beer after it has been automatically put into the bottles, guarantees the lasting purity of our product. We bottle all our beer at the brewery in clear crystal bottles, showing at a glance its cleanliness and brilliancy. Delivered direct to all licensed dealers in steel cases.

JACOB RUPPERT, Brewer.
Third Ave., 90th to 93rd St

1912

BLATZ
MIWAUKEE

THE FINEST BEER EVER BREWED

Go to the phone <u>now</u> and order a case of Blatz—<u>the</u> beer that should be in every household where a superior malt beverage is desired.

Generations ago Blatz was brewed by an old fashioned brewer in a primitive fashion. Today the methods are modern and original, and the capacity of the plant is enormous, but the <u>quality</u> and <u>character</u> of the product remain the same as of old.

Taylor & Edgington, *Distributers*
Williams, Ariz.

ALWAYS THE SAME GOOD OLD

Blatz

97

"To the health of Utah"

Utah People Should Drink Beers That Are Brewed in Utah

This is the first of a series of seven articles. One will appear each day this week. We want you to read every one of them. It's to your interest.

You should drink Utah beers in preference to all others, not only because they are HOME PRODUCTS, but because there are no better beers brewed anywhere. Highest quality at moderate cost.

Each of the Utah beers is full of life and snap, with an individual flavor all its own. They are prepared from selected barley and hops in up-to-date, sanitary breweries, where every law regarding purity and cleanliness is observed.

The three breweries of Salt Lake City employ hundreds of skilled workmen; they purchase from Utah farmers tens of thousands of dollars' worth of raw material annually.

They expend with dealers and tradesmen in Salt Lake a small fortune each year and contribute a large share toward the expense of city, county and state government. They are real builders.

Whether in the home, at the hotel, club, buffet or the restaurant, every loyal Utahn will insist upon Utah beers. Each beer is a healthful, appetizing, nourishing drink. Any doctor will tell you that a moderate use of beer is beneficial. Be sure that the beer you drink is brewed in Utah.

Brewed and Bottled at the Breweries in Salt Lake

THE SALT LAKE TRIBUNE (UTAH), MARCH 31, 1912

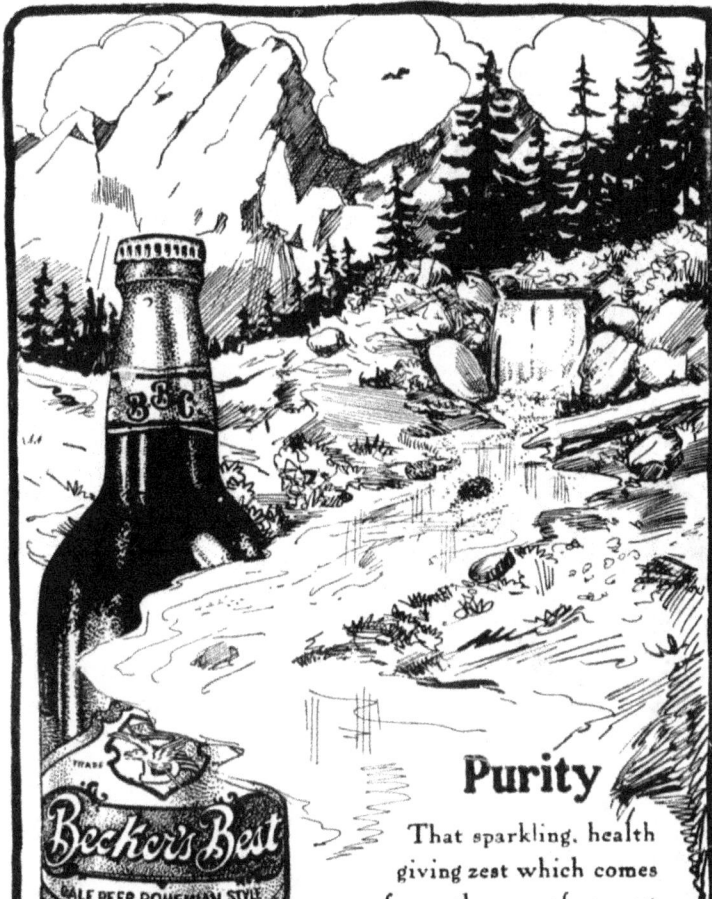

Purity

That sparkling, health giving zest which comes from the use of purest mountain brook water in the brewing of Becker's Beer. "Better by test than all the rest."

Becker's Best

The beer for all— The true health food beverage—for table use — or between meals—nourishing— satisfying.

Write for price list—Order Direct from

Becker Brewing & Malting Co.
OGDEN. UTAH.

H.P.Co

GOODWIN'S WEEKLY (UTAH), MAY 18, 1912

Physical fitness

—the co-ordinate action of brain and muscle, the healthy condition of all the organs of the body are assured, if BECKER'S BEST is the beverage—at meals or between meals.

Write for Price List
ORDER DIRECT FROM

Becker Brewing & Malting Co. Ogden, Utah.

HPG

GOODWIN'S WEEKLY (UTAH), OCT 05, 1912

1912

Write or Phone

Write or Phone for a case of

Both Phones 159

Everett BEER

Both Phones 159

Delivered to your home for $2.00 per case for Pints.
$3.20 per case for Quarts.
50c. rebate for return of case and bottles

Everett Brewing Company

The Perfect Product of a Great Plant

We have a just pride in the size of the great Pabst Brewery, in the completeness of the equipment, in the skill of the brewers and in the perfection of the Pabst brewing methods.

We have more pride in the perfect product of this great brewery — *Pabst Blue Ribbon,* The Beer of Quality — a beer of absolute purity, sparkle, delicate flavor and delightful smoothness.

PABST BREWING COMPANY, MILWAUKEE, WIS.

MACFARLANE & COMPANY, Ltd., DISTRIBUTORS

Phone 2026

P. O. Box 488

Beer Exposed to Light for 5 Minutes Becomes Undrinkable

This is not our statement, but the deliberate opinion of one of the most renowned scientists in the world. Read the entire statement:

"We have tested beers repeatedly, placing the bottles in the direct sunlight, and testing the same after one, two, three and five minutes exposure, found that the beer with three and five minutes exposure became undrinkable on account of the peculiar odor developed. The detrimental effect of light upon beer can be successfully counteracted by the employment of brown or dark colored glass bottles, and such bottles are, therefore, recommendable." — *Wahl-Henius Institute of Fermentology.*

It is not enough that beer be brewed pure, it must be kept pure.

Many Americans prefer beer in a light bottle. Most brewers follow the course of least resistance.

Light starts decay even in pure beer. Dark glass gives the best protection against light. Schlitz is sold in Brown Bottles to protect its purity from the brewery to your glass.

See that cream or cork is branded "Schlitz."

Schlitz
The Beer That Made Milwaukee Famous.

THE NATIONAL DRINK

—The sturdy German people are noted for their domestic simplicity in home life.

—The American people are fast recognizing the Teutonic diet and are speedily adopting it

Our "OLD GERMAN LAGER"

adds zest and relish to the plainest meal. It is a food in itself, and is entirely different from any beer you have tasted.

—It has that Imported Flavor.

Phone Hyland 17

Brewed and bottled only by

THE SALT LAKE CITY BREWING COMPANY

Brewers of "Old German Lager," and American Beauty Beers.

THE F&M Schaefer Wiener Style Beer

Wholesome Delicious Nutritious

BREWERY BOTTLING

Order a Case
Tel. 170—Plaza

OLDEST LAGER BEER BREWERY IN AMERICA.

THE WILLIAMS NEWS (ARIZONA), MAY 11, 1912

1912

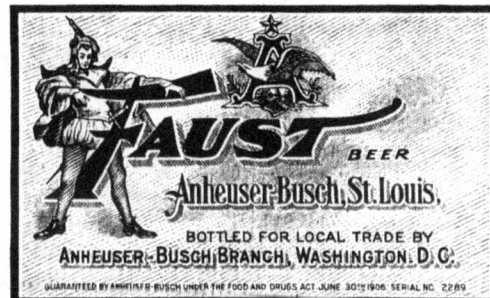

THE WILLIAMS NEWS (ARIZONA), JUNE 22, 1912   THE WASHINGTON TIMES, MAY 25, 1912

Schlitz Brown Bottle Is Making History

Two years ago, Schlitz adopted the Brown Bottle.

Scientists, world famous, had rendered opinions that beer exposed to light cannot remain pure.

One year ago, Schlitz corroborated its claims by reprinting such parts of these opinions as were pertinent.

Today, the last link in this long chain of incontrovertible evidence is complete.

We reproduce herewith in miniature the printed matter on covers or caution cards taken from cases of beer sold by brewers using the light bottle.

Read them.

They are self-explanatory. They are eloquent.

These competitors admit the weakness of their own product when exposed to light, by warning the public to "Keep the cover on."

Phones N. 2171—2172
Jos. Schlitz Brewing Co.
3d & Randolph Place, N. E.
Washington, D. C.

Schlitz
The Beer That Made Milwaukee Famous.

The result of good brewing—

Careful selection of materials — a generous amount to each brew, never less — proper aging in wood, an indispensable feature of good brewing — up to the minute, absolutely cleanly bottling methods — have won for HIGH LIFE the distinction of being the most wholesome and *"Finest tasting beer ever produced."* Convince yourself — order a case today.

We use light bottles exclusively for this high grade beer — common beer comes in dark bottles

THE BROWN BOTTLE JOKE

The brown bottle fallacy has been so completely exploded that little is left to be said in defense of that side of the question which advocated the use of dark bottles to the absolute exclusion of light bottles. It is admitted that common beer comes in dark bottles and that beer of a high degree of stability is preferably bottled in light bottles.

Wahl-Henius Institute of Fermentology (America's greatest authorities on brewing) are in accord with this view. Here is their statement in relation to the bottling of high-grade beer:

"FOR SUCH BEERS THE LIGHT BOTTLE is PREFERABLY EMPLOYED because it can more readily be inspected before filling to insure thorough cleanliness, and because the finished package reveals at a glance whether the contents meet the requirements of the consumer as to color, clarity and freedom from sedimentation."

Miller HIGH LIFE

The Champagne of Bottled Beer

Brewed in Milwaukee by Miller Brewing Co.

On sale at leading Buffets, on Dining Cars and Steam ship Lines.

HIGH LIFE in Germany

Why Drink Water When You Can Get Salem Beer?

The Most Popular Beverage on the Pacific Coast

Salem Bottled Beer is brewed in one of the most modern plants on the Pacific Coast. It is aged in steel glass-lined tanks. It is conveyed by modern pipe line system direct to the bottle house, bottled under pressure and never comes in contact with the air from the time it leaves the fermenting tank until the bottle is opened by the consumer. Therefore the consumer is absolutely assured a beer of ideal effervescence, snap and purity. A trial will surely convince you. Get it from your local dealer or send order to the

Salem Brewery Association

Salem, Oregon

DAILY CAPITAL JOURNAL (SALEM, OREGON), SEPTEMBER 29, 1913

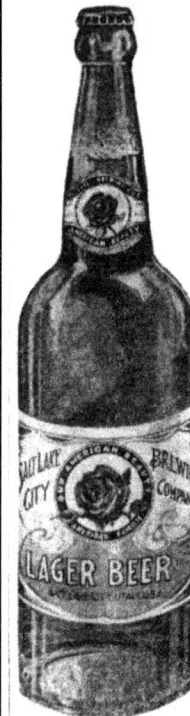

1913

DRINK....

AMERICAN BEAUTY

....BEER

Those who have tried it will tell you that it is the finest beer brewed.

"A Stream of Throat Delight"

It is made from the finest imported Bohemian hops, sparkling spring water and best Utah Club barley used exclusively in its manufacture. Try a case, then you be the judge.

Salt Lake City Brewing Co.

——

GEO. BANOVICH
DISTRIBUTOR
TONOPAH, NEV.

TONOPAH DAILY BONANZA (NV), SEPTEMBER 11, 1913

DAS GUTE BIER

Our DOUBLE INSPECTION Guarantees Purity

Perfect Brew

A Guarantee Impossible With the Brown Bottle

Perfect Brew is always sold in clear glass bottles to insure absolute purity and cleanliness. Our rule is to see that every bottle before it is refilled with "PERFECT BREW" is absolutely clean----examined after washing and again after it is filled and pasteurized.

Perfect Brew is NOT affected by light, as it is a well-brewed and well-aged beer.

In making "Perfect Brew" ours has been a persistent purpose to produce a perfect beer so perfect in materials, fermentation, aging, and bottling that we conscientiously offer you a faultless hop and malt beverage.

"Ask for a Bottle."   "Have a Case Sent Home."
At Any Hotel, Club, or Cafe.
From Wholesalers and Grocers Everywhere.

"One Bottle Will Convince You"
MONUMENTAL BREWING CO.,
7th and Rhode Island Avenue N. E.

THE WASHINGTON HERALD, SEPTEMBER 05, 1913

Caps the Climax

of Quality Purity and Flavor

Every drop of Blue Ribbon is perfect in purity, quality and flavor—all that beer *should* be—all that the best beer *can* be—beneficial and delicious. For

Pabst
Blue Ribbon
The Beer of Quality

is brewed and bottled with the skill and care that *perfects* and *protects* its *purity*,—its goodness. Comes out of the bottle just as it goes in—a crystal clear, bubbling, sparkling beverage, good to look at—good to drink. Try it and you'll like beer better than ever before.

Arizona Mercantile Co.
Tel. 1068
Center & Adams Sts.   PHOENIX, ARIZ.

Copyright 1914, Pabst Brewing Co.

YOUR best friends, like our best friends, are those who are <u>always</u> the <u>same</u>—not angels yesterday and grouches to-day, but the same dependable good souls every day alike.

Day after day and year after year our Liebotschaner is the same uniformly fine and delectable brew that it always was.

So, since it is true that even nature never makes two leaves or anything else exactly alike, would you blame us for being a bit proud.

Liebotschaner

Pure Beer in its highest expression.

Genesee Brewing Co.
Phones 71.

DEMOCRAT AND CHRONICLE (ROCHESTER, NY)
JANUARY 14, 1912

You don't need a pencil to figure this:

Your doctor's fees are $2.00 (or more) per visit on each case. Our Liebotschaner is $1.40 (no more) per case---24 bottles.

Quite a number of people---about 30,000 in our own city---see the point, but of course if you prefer to employ the doctor, it would be quite a mistake to spend the money for

Liebotschaner

One bottle at mealtimes---and *watch!*

Genesee Brewing Co.
Phones 71.

DEMOCRAT AND CHRONICLE (ROCHESTER, NY)
JANUARY 24, 1912

Detroit Brewing Co's

1913

Detroit-Bohemian Beer

Detroits leading physicians prescribe pure beer for people who need a tonic.

Detroit Bohemian Beer is a favorite with many eminent doctors because of its known purity, high food value and delicious flavor.

That wonderful "tang," so beneficial to poor appetite, comes from the Genuine Saazer Hops which we import from Old Bohemia.

Detroit-Bohemian Beer Never Causes a Headache.
Order a Case by Phone.
Call Main 5528 or City 11.

DETROIT BREWING CO.

DETROIT FREE PRESS (MICHIGAN), JANUARY 3, 1912

108

109

EVENING CAPITAL NEWS (BOISE, IDAHO), JANUARY 05, 1913

111

Wonderful Invention Gives
Americans "A Draught Beer in Bottles"

THE KIESELGUHR
SILVER PLATED
FILTER
Four Feet in Diameter

Comprising 254 filter tubes
of Kieselguhr or diatoma-
cious earth. Each tube
3 inches in diameter and 16
inches long.

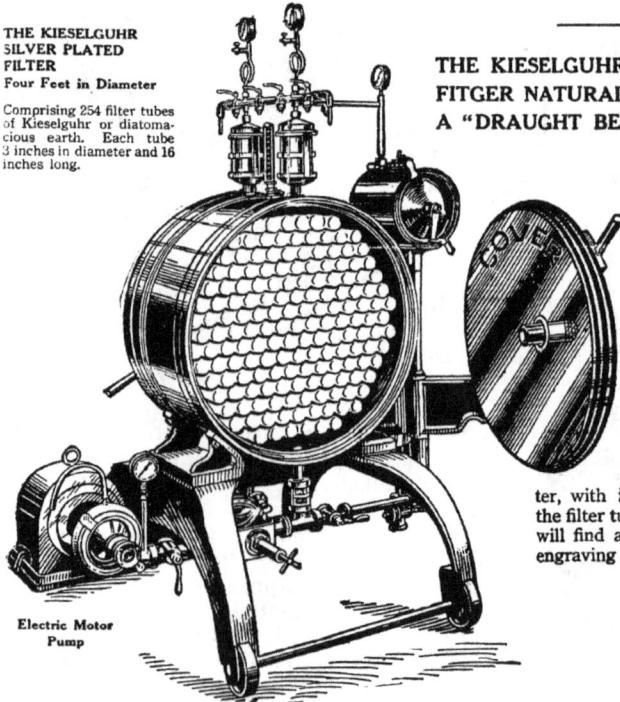

Electric Motor
Pump

THE KIESELGUHR FILTER MAKES FITGER NATURAL BEER A "DRAUGHT BEER IN BOTTLES"

This wonderful invention completely corrects the evils of pasteurization, in fact it does by filtration what others are doing by pasteurization and the natural results is a natural beer, thus ours is no just-as-good method, but a better one, a perfect one.

This picture of our silver-plated filter, with its cover open, shows the filter tubes in position. You will find a more complete steel engraving in every case.

Fitger Natural Beer, filtered by the Kieselguhr filter, has the wonderful natural taste and aroma of the *finest beer as drawn from the wood*.

The Fitger Kieselguhr filter (first of its kind in America) takes the place of pasteurization, the process used by other brewers for "keeping" bottled beer.

Pasteurization does not preserve the natural taste of beer. Kieselguhr filtration is the only known way to "keep" beer in bottles and preserve its natural taste. For this reason all brewers will in time use Kieselguhr filtration.

Kieselguhr filtration makes Fitger Natural Beer the clearest, most brilliant beer in America.

A. Fitger

FITGER Natural Beer
"A Draught Beer in Bottles"

Besides being the purest and most brilliant beer in America, Fitger Natural Beer is the equal in quality of any beer made in Europe. The truth of this and of our claim that it is

"The Most Brilliant Beer in America"

is proved in the drinking of it, a pleasure easily within the reach of all.

FITGER BREWING COMPANY, DULUTH, MINN.

ABOVE: THE BEMIDJI DAILY PIONEER (MN), DECEMBER 18, 1914

1914

RIGHT TOP: OMAHA DAILY BEE (NEBRASKA), MAY 07, 1914

RIGHT MIDDLE: THE LABOR WORLD (MN), NOVEMBER 14, 1914

RIGHT BOTTOM: THE WASHINGTON TIMES (DC), AUGUST 12, 1914

113

FOOD-TEMPERANCE-AND BEER

"The purpose of this advertisement is not to induce people to drink more beer, but to influence more people to drink beer."

Good beer, properly brewed, is the greatest aid to true temperance.

Everybody should drink good beer, because it is wholesome and nutritious. It is the purest of foods—in liquid form. It stimulates the appetite, aids digestion and is an ideal temperate beverage.

Prof. Gaertner in his "Manual of Hygiene" says that one quart of beer is equal in food value to 3/10 pound of bread in carbo-hydrates and two ounces of bread or nearly one ounce of meat in albumen.

Heavy foods clog the system and cause many ills.

Physicians and food experts throughout the world advocate the drinking of good, wholesome beer for its nutritive value and purity.

The great nations of Europe furnish beer to their soldiers and sailors with their meals.

College and professional athletes are allowed to drink beer while in training.

Beer, bottled at the brewery, is absolutely pure, being entirely free from the disease bearing germs frequently found in milk and water. The greatest vigilance is observed in a brewery to keep every nook and corner scrupulously clean in order to minimize the dangers of contamination. It is the one beverage that cannot be adulterated or tampered with from the time it leaves the brewery until it reaches the consumer.

We have developed to the utmost degree the nutritive qualities and purity of

RUPPERT'S
Knickerbocker
The Beer That Satisfies

It is made of the highest grade Barley-Malt and the finest quality Saazer Hops.

Throughout all the various processes of brewing, filtering, aging, bottling and pasteurization, it is constantly watched over and inspected by experts. It is absolutely pure when it leaves the brewery, and must be absolutely pure when it reaches you.

The public is cordially invited to call and inspect our Brewery and Bottling Department. It is the most modern and best equipped brewhouse on earth.

The Jacob Ruppert Brewery
Third Avenue, 90th to 92d Street — NEW YORK

JACOB RUPPERT
Knickerbocker Beer
BREWERY BOTTLING
3RD AVE. 90TH TO 92TH STREET

THE EVENING WORLD (NEW YORK NY), SEPTEMBER 22, 1914

1914

Jacob Ruppert, Jr. inherited this successful brewery from his father in 1915. Later that year, Jacob Junior used some of his new wealth to buy the New York Yankees baseball team. Both of these business ventures ended up being very profitable.

Beer Is The Greatest Beverage Made By Man

WHY IS IT that beer remains the world's greatest manufactured beverage in spite of the endeavors of science and vast appropriations of money to produce "soft" and other drinks to take its place? There is only one reason—Beer is the purest, most healthful and satisfying beverage for all occasions.

Fitger's Beer

30 Years the Choice.

The real goodness of bear is demonstrated in Fitger's. It combines all the valuable qualities of other good beers with a peculiarly delicious flavor produced only by the Fitger process. Try a case in your home. That's the best test.

FITGER BREWING CO., DULUTH, MINN.

ABOVE: THE VIRGINIA ENTERPRISE, SEPTEMBER 18, 1914

"When the Evening Whistle Blows."

After the long day's work —work in wood, leather, flint or stone dust—dust that burns and chokes, **you** may **demand** and **need** a pure and nutritious beverage. Hoosier Cream, Tiger Export Beer, the drink of the temperate, will nourish and rest you.

Brewery Bottled.

SOUTH BEND BREWING ASSOCIATION

Servant to Lovers of Good Beer.

SOUTH BEND NEWS-TIMES (IN), OCTOBER 08, 1914

GOOD BEER IS HEALTHFUL
—but be sure it IS good—Insist on
DAISY BEER

It contains all the ingredients of GOOD, WHOLESOME BEER— selected hops, best malt and pure water.

It is brewed by skilled men under the best sanitary conditions—men who produce nothing but Beer of the highest quality and finest flavor.

This is the Beer for you and your family—

DAISY

Brewed and Bottled by
GLOBE BREWERY
Monongahela, Pa.
Of
Independent Brewing Company
of Pittsburgh, Pa.

THE DAILY REPUBLICAN (AZ), JAN 9, 1914

115

THE WIBAUX PIONEER (WI), JUNE 12, 1914   THE HERALD (NEW ORLEANS, LA), SEPTEMBER 24, 1914

This Beer is Better

Pabst Blue Ribbon
The Beer of Quality

is better because of its Age, Strength and Purity. The soft smoothness of Blue Ribbon is agreeable to everybody. It has the full flavor of fully matured malt, so plainly noticeable, and a zestful snap which is extremely enjoyable.

Beneath its rich, creamy foam you will find a mellow, delicious beverage that not only satisfies as a drink but is a natural tonic—pure, wholesome and nourishing.

Pabst Blue Ribbon is better beer because it possesses all that is best in beer.

The Meyers Co., Inc.
Telephone 125
110 West Silver Ave.   ALBUQUERQUE, N. M.

CLEANLINESS AND TEMPERANCE PREVENT DISEASE

Beer is a beverage conducive to health. It works in the direction of moderation and true temperance.

Beer is absolutely pure, being entirely free from disease-bearing germs so frequently found in milk and water.

"The milk and butter men of Indiana ought to visit the breweries of this and other states", said Mr. H. E. Barnard, State Food and Drug Commissioner of Indiana, "in order to see how clean a food establishment may be made. It is a fact that the cleanest and most sanitary food on the market, as food is described by the Indiana law, is beer."

"What is good for the breweries is good for the babies" said Dr. P. M. Hall of Minneapolis, in advocating the adoption of brewery methods in the handling of milk.

1914

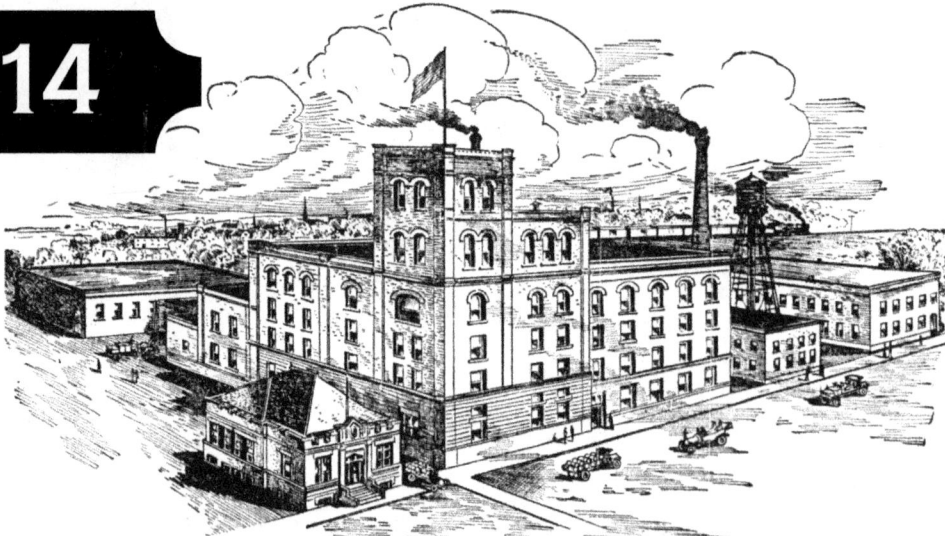

New Plant—Muessel Brewing Co.
CAPACITY __ 200,000 BARRELS. __

The most up-to-date brewing plant in the United States

Beer has received the hearty indorsement of leading medical and scientific authorities the world over.

"Beer is a veritable food product", says Dr. Wiley, the U. S. expert on pure foods.

Liebig, the famous German chemist, described beer as "liquid bread".

The eminent scientist, Pasteur earnestly advocated the regular use of beer.

"Beer is a refreshing, exhilarating nutritive. A light beer, well flavored with the hop, is calculated to promote digestion and may be relied upon as constituting one of the most wholesome of beverages"—Dr. F. W. Pavy, Fellow of the Royal College of Physicians, London.

THE MUESSEL BREWING CO.

CLOCKWISE FROM UPPER LEFT:

ESCANABA MORNING PRESS
(MICHIGAN), JAN 17, 1914

JANESVILLE DAILY GAZETTE
(WISCONSIN), AUGUST 1, 1914

DETROIT FREE PRESS
(MICHIGAN), AUGUST 20, 1914

FORT WAYNE DAILY NEWS
(INDIANA), MARCH 11, 1914

THE EVENING WORLD (NEW YORK NY), OCTOBER 24, 1914

BOTH ADS AT RIGHT: GOODWIN'S WEEKLY (UTAH), OCTOBER 17, 1914

5,000 Years to Produce Beer of Centlivre Quality

History records the brewing of beer (barley wine) in Egypt over 5,000 years ago.

Since that time the history of the industry has been one of continual betterment—better methods and facilities and a better product.

A modern exponent of all that is best in brewing is the brewery of the C. L. Centlivre Brewing Co.—the home of Nickel Plate Beer.

This brewery represents the crystalized thought, effort and money that has been given to the industry for ages past—it represents the skill and genius of many specialists, experts and engineers—an equipment procured in Europe and America.

And from this better brewery comes a better beer—Nickel Plate Beer—a beer brewed from the finest materials, aged to full ripe maturity—then freshly tapped, bottled at the brewery and promptly delivered before it has lost any of its goodness—pure, palatable, healthful—the soul of golden barley malt and aromatic hops.

1914 *Centlivre Beer*

IT MAKES FRIENDS

THE IDEAL BEVERAGE FOR THE HOME
KEEP A CASE IN YOUR REFRIGERATOR.   PHONES 42 AND 62

Beer Storage Cellar

NEW beer is not good to drink and a number of brewers put their product on the market much too soon.

Good beer deserves to be properly aged and for that reason the ageing process for

Tech Beer

gets especial care.

After leaving the fermentation tanks the beer is piped into the storage cellars where immense tanks are provided for its reception.

Here the beer is kept at a very low temperature while the secondary fermentation of ageing takes place. During this time certain albuminous bodies, which, if left in the beer would make it cloudy, are separated and precipitated by the low temperature. The beer is now comparatively clear.

Follows, certain changes in the component parts of the beer and a rare, aromatic flavor is acquired in the storage tanks.

Tech Beer is properly aged.

Ample capital and abundant storage capacity enable this company to properly age every drop of beer and TECH does not suffer in this respect, being kept in storage at least six months before it is ready for the final processes.

TECH BEER can be safely and wisely taken by the most delicate, by those who have to exercise the greatest care regarding both food and drink as it is easily and quickly digested. TECH will not cause biliousness which so often follows the drinking of immature and improperly-aged beer.

If you wish a perfect beverage, rich in nutriment and deliciously flavored try TECH.

All good dealers supply TECH BEER for home trade.

Phone your dealer for a case today.

Pittsburgh Brewing Company

No. 11 will explain the next step—The ship cask process—an interesting method of fining the beer.

Old Mission Lager Beer

TRADITIONALLY GOOD

1912

1769

1914

TO THOSE WHO PREFER

Quality to Quantity

WE HAVE IN

Old Mission Lager

TRADITIONALLY GOOD

Something to offer to Consumers which will at once awaken the sense of taste to a keen appreciation of the difference between an ordinary Beer and one which possesses the finish and refined after-taste, which can only be attained by the utilization of specially selected materials, with water that possesses properties especially adapted to brewing purposes, in the hands of a skilled Brewmaster.

You Therefore Find In

OLD MISSION LAGER

Beer, all of these requisites which establishes its high standard, and is the peer of the World's Best Brews.

Give this celebrated beer a trial at your Club, Cafe or Bar, or have your dealer send a case to the home. Please accept no substitutes, and should your dealer offer you something "Just as Good," or will not supply you, phone up our Family Liquor Department, No. 1057, and your order will be promptly executed.

Unity Commercial Company

Wholsale Distributors

Telephone 1057

40 South Central

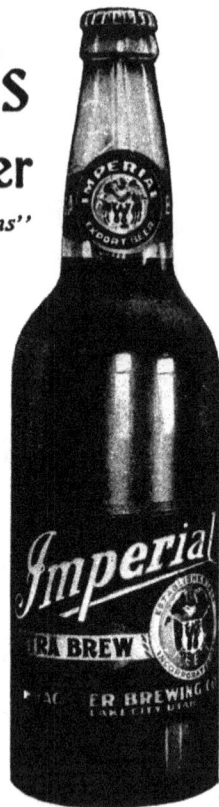

ABOVE: EVENING STAR (WASHINGTON DC), MARCH 07, 1914

ON THE RIGHT, TOP TO BOTTOM:

THE VIRGINIA ENTERPRISE (VIRGINIA), JANUARY 09, 1914
OMAHA DAILY BEE (NEBRASKA), FEBRUARY 11, 1914
EVENING STAR (WASHINGTON DC), APRIL 28, 1914

BELOW: BISBEE DAILY REVIEW (ARIZONA), MARCH 26, 1914

Food for Thought

HERE is a beer for brain workers as well as for men of brawn. It possesses all the elements that impart vigor to the system, aid the tired brain and strengthen the nerves as well as producing bone and muscle.

All the nutritive ingredients of a perfect beer are found to the highest degree in

Hamm's BEER

The brainiest men of almost all nations have been consistent beer drinkers. The deepest thinking scientists and pure food experts have endorsed beer as a wholesome food product.

THEO. HAMM BREWING CO.
ST. PAUL

The End of a Perfect Day

Eventide is one of the sweetest words in our language. To the laborer it means relief from the day's toil; to the man of affairs it means respite from the keen strife of business. It means the return to that haven of rest—the home.

To the housewife it means her hour of triumph when she may gather around her those for whom she has made home a place of contentment. The evening meal is to her an occasion of cheer. How well she has planned if a part of that meal is a bottle of

Hamm's BEER

It is an adjunct to the perfect closing of a perfect day.

THEO. HAMM BREWING CO.
ST. PAUL

BOTH ADS ABOVE:

THE APPEAL
(ST PAUL, MINNESOTA)
OCTOBER 16, 1915

RIGHT:
THE WASHINGTON
HERALD (DC)
AUGUST 20, 1915

1915

Anheuser-Busch's

Faust Beer

A DELICIOUSLY flavored Barley— Malt and Hop Beer brewed and aged in the world's most celebrated brewery.

Delivered to your home at $1.80 per case of two dozen bottles.

At clubs, hotels, cafes and bars, 10c per bottle.

Brewed at the
Anheuser-Busch Brewery
St. Louis

Anheuser-Busch Branch
Distributors   WASHINGTON, D. C.

128

A Comfort in Your Home

USE the same good judgment in choosing your beer as you do in buying your food, milk and water.

For carefully selected bottled beer will be a source of great comfort, health and enjoyment in your home.

Order Green Seal—the best, purest and safest bottled beer it is possible to buy.

Physicians prescribe it for nursing mothers, so it must be good for you. It is made of the finest materials the market affords. It is brewed and bottled under absolutely sanitary conditions.

Always keep a bottle or two of Green Seal Beer in your ice box. Nothing else goes so far at such a reasonable cost.

Temperance Talks

Beer drinkers constitute a class by themselves. They are not attracted by whiskey and brandy.

They have a normal taste for a beverage which quenches their thirst and at the same time supplies in a considerable measure, the nourishment which is derived from meat and bread. They do not drink beer for the alcohol it contains.

A gallon of 3½ per cent beer has only 4½ ounces of alcohol. You will agree that very few people possess the capacity to drink such a quantity daily.

Yet this is equivalent in alcoholic contents to 3 or 4 small drinks of whiskey.

John Sackman
Fairfield Ave. and
Wabash R. R.
Phone—Home 6435.

24 Large or 36 Small
Bottles in Cases

Green Seal Bottled Beer

The Buckeye Brewing Co., Toledo, O.

Not Delivered in Cases of 24 Large or 36 Small Bottles

129

THE DAGUERROTYPE: May 9th, 1840: A most important consummation has been attained in this wonderful art. In Philadelphia, likenesses of the human face have been taken by it. The resemblance is divine.

1840 — 1915

Seventy five years ago

before the days of photography, the firm of Lemp was brewing fine beers — the oldest brewery in America with a national patronage.

The "practice that makes perfect" has brought to Americans of today, the unrivaled flavor of

"She choicest product of the brewer's art"

FALSTAFF

Compare it with no other beer; for its flavor is its own—delightfully, wholly *Falstaff*.

Beer is a food. Bread and beer are made of the same materials; cereals, yeast and water. Bread is solid; beer is liquid—both are highly nourishing. Physicians prescribe beer to produce energy, build tissue and strengthen nerves. Good beer is the elixir of life.

Henry Rohlff Company, Distributor, 2567-69 Leavenworth St., Omaha, Neb.
Telephone: Doug. 876

FALSTAFF BOTTLED BEER — WM. J. LEMP BREWING CO. ST. LOUIS, U.S.A.

OMAHA DAILY BEE (NEBRASKA), FEBRUARY 05, 1915

When you drink Beer you will want the best —so be safe by specifying either

American Beauty

or our

Regal Lager Beers

Order a case from your dealer or phone Hy. 17

Salt Lake City Brewing Co.

Brewed from Choicest Materials — REGAL LAGER BEER — SALT LAKE CITY BREWING CO. SALT LAKE CITY, UTAH

GOODWIN'S WEEKLY (UTAH), MAY 08, 1915

"Quality in it Every Minute."

Hamm's BEER

MOST MODERN BOTTLING PLANT

THEO. HAMM BREWING CO. ST. PAUL

THE APPEAL (MINNESOTA), APRIL 03, 1915

CALL SUPERIOR 645

Prima BEER

"24 GOOD REASONS"

PHONE CANAL 9—The "Edelweiss" Line
FOR

Edelweiss BEER

A CASE OF GOOD JUDGMENT

Copyright 1911 by the P. Schoenhofen Brewing Co.

CHICAGO EAGLE (ILLINOIS), JANUARY 30, 1915

131

Benj. Franklin Nourished With Beer

AUTHOR OF "POOR RICHARD" UNDERSTOOD *REAL* TEMPERANCE

BENJAMIN FRANKLIN

Philosopher and Statesman, signer of the Declaration of Independence. Founder of American Philosophical Society, 1743. Ambassador to France, 1776-85.

Benjamin Franklin says, "Be sober and temperate and you will be healthy."

It is Franklin who, in the story of his early struggles, tells how, with a room-mate in London, he subsisted upon "only half an anchovy each, on a very little strip of bread, and half a pint of ale between us."

This well-loved American, whose wineglass is still treasured by the Historical Society of Pennsylvania, lived to the good age of 84. At 81 he received a visit from the Rev. Manasseh Cutler who records in his journal that he "was delighted with the vivacity of his mental faculties notwithstanding his age."

The barley brews and light wines used by Franklin have their modern equivalent in natural beer.

DULUTH GIVES THE WORLD A "DRAUGHT BEER IN BOTTLES"

A draught beer in bottles has come at last. Kieselguhr filtration, the simple process of filtering the natural beer through Kieselguhr filters, gives to the world that supposed paradox, *"a draught beer in bottles."*

Who has not noted the difference between the rich, creamy beers drawn from wood in a Rathskeller and the flat, tastelessness of pasteurized beer in bottles?

Fitger Natural Beer in bottles is Natural, like the creamy brews of a Rathskeller. It has all the fragrance, rich character and indescribable taste of pungent hops and wholesome barley malt that characterizes the richest brews as drawn fresh from the wood. It has, besides, *a crystal purity and sparkling brilliancy that unfiltered beer cannot possess.*

A. Fitger

FITGER Natural Beer
"A Draught Beer in Bottles"

We wish to point out that physicians generally concur in the opinion that small quantities of pure beer stimulate appetite and aid digestion. As an adjunct to a meal there is nothing pleasanter or more beneficial than

"The Most Brilliant Beer in America"
FITGER BREWING COMPANY, DULUTH, MINN.

Telephone 621 Douglas — TIVOLI BREWING CO. Detroit, Mich.

Altes Lager
The Beer in the Green Bottle

THE FAMOUS CREAM OF MALT BEER
IS BREWED SOLELY BY THE

J. L. Hoerber Brewing Company
1617 to 1619 21st Place
Telephone Canal 138
CHICAGO

1915

Here's a beer *de Luxe* — a beer brewed from selected barley malt and choicest Bohemian hops—a beer that *thousands* select because of its *flavor.*

Goetz Country Club

Chill won't make it bitter. Chill-proofed by our own exclusive process, sold at all first-class bars and restaurants. Ask for Goetz.

Save the Labels. Send for our Premium List.
M. K. GOETZ BREWING CO., St. Joseph, Mo.

Alexander Hamilton Encouraged Brewing.

FIRST CONGRESS A UNIT IN THE OPINION THAT BREWING DESERVES SPECIAL ENCOURAGEMENT.

In 1789 Alexander Hamilton introduced a revenue system with the object of encouraging the industry of brewing for moral and hygienic reasons. His efforts were supported by the First Congress which moved that if "The morals of the people are to be improved by whatever enters their diet, it would be prudent of the National Legislature to *encourage the manufacture of malt liquors.*"

Dr. Benjamin Rush, father of real temperance, famous publicist and professor of medicine, taught that the promotion of temperance could be accomplished only by the encouragement of the brewing industry.

ALEXANDER HAMILTON

Upon every clause of the constitution of the United States his individuality is indelibly stamped. Daniel Webster says of him: "He smote the rock of national resources and abundant streams of revenue gushed forth."

FITGER NATURAL BEER IS A SPARKLING DRAUGHT BEER—BUT BOTTLED

It is draught beer *because it has the full natural character taste and aroma of the best beer as drawn from the wood.* Heretofore the only known way to keep bottled beer was by pasteurization. Pasteurization, or steaming, gives beer that noticeable flatness of taste. heretofore the great objection to bottled beer.

Kieselguhr filtration our new process keeps bottled beer better than pasteurization. It filters beer to a pure brilliancy heretofore unknown. It preserves in Fitger Natural Beer all the qualities that heretofore have made draught beer preferable to bottled.

Our *Kieselguhr filter* is the first of its kind in America.

A. Fitger

FITGER Natural Beer
"A Draught Beer in Bottles"

Fitger Natural Beer does more than please the palate. Dr. F. W. Pavy, Fellow of the Royal College of Physicians, London, says: "Beer is a refreshing, exhilarating nutritive. A light beer well flavored with hops is calculated to promote digestion." The tonic-hops properties are very marked in

"The Most Brilliant Beer in America"
FITGER BREWING COMPANY, DULUTH, MINN.

PURPLE LABEL

GREEN LABEL

Hanley's Brewery Bottling
and what it means to you.

Our responsibility does not end with the brewing of Hanley's Peerless Ales.

To make perfect ales is but part of the function of The James Hanley Brewing Company.

To deliver these perfect ales in perfect condition is equally important.

In bottled goods we accomplish this by maintaining one of the most modern, sanitary and highly efficient Brewery Bottling plants in the world.

Brewery Bottling Brew is run direct from government storage tanks into cleansed and sterilized bottles. Every bottle is hermetically crowned; no contamination can get in and no goodness can get out.

The dark glass keeps out light.

Thoro pasteurization safe-guards the contents against changes of temperature.

The ale reaches you in the same condition it leaves our storage vats.

Finally as an unmistakable mark of identification the trade mark "ALE" is used only on Brewery Bottling Brew labels.

The color of the label tells the kind of brew: Dark, Pale, Halfstock, Extra or Porter.
Learn to distinguish them and order your favorite kind.

The Brewery Bottling Brew costs you no more than the ordinary bottling of ordinary bulk Ale. . . . . Order from your Dealer.

THE JAMES HANLEY BREWING CO.
PROVIDENCE,   RHODE ISLAND
Brewers and Bottlers of Ale and Porter Exclusively.

BLUE LABEL

RED LABEL

HANLEY'S ALE PEERLESS
The Standard of Excellence

NORWICH BULLETIN (CT), AUGUST 19, 1915

A True Blue American

that enjoys a bottle of

Blatz

MILWAUKEE'S MOST EXQUISITE

BEER

Beer Best Brain Food, Says Prof. Chandler

And It's Never Adulterated, So Columbia Man Tells Master Brewers' Convention

Prof. Charles Frederick Chandler is the ranking Professor of Chemistry at Columbia University, New York City, the largest University in the world.

"Beer," said Prof. Chandler, "is a beverage prepared from barley, water, hops and yeast. Beer is food. American beer contains 6 per cent. solid food, only 3 to 4 per cent. alcohol and also lecithin, which is real brain food. Beer and bread are both made from cereals; bread with water and is solid; beer with more water and is liquid. Yeast converts both into palatable and readily digested food. Both contain alcohol. Beer is not intoxicating in ordinary quantities and beer is one of the foods that is free from bacteria. It is appetizing and aids digestion. I have had some experience with beer and have been a consumer. I have enjoyed most perfect health and I guess I am a pretty good specimen of the food value of beer.

"I don't believe there is any beer made in the United States that is what you call adulterated. It may be misbranded, but not adulterated. If the prohibitionists drive beer from the household they will deprive a large part of the population of a wholesome article of food. There you have reasons enough why beer has become our national beverage."

(N. Y. Sun, Oct. 6, 1914).

Nothing Else Will Satisfy Him

Popular—that's the word with *all* true Americans—with *all* classes—physicians, laborers, mechanics, bankers, business men.

Blatz Beer is best in quality, taste and purity—Good for you—Good for your friends.

Pure, wholesome, snappy and individual in taste. If you have been drinking other beers, it's because you have never tasted BLATZ

Order a Case so You and Your Friends Can Enjoy it

VAL. BLATZ BREWING CO., MILWAUKEE

BLATZ COMPANY
802-810 Douglas   OMAHA, NEBR.

Phone Douglas 6662

OMAHA DAILY BEE (NEBRASKA), MAY 06, 1915

Domestic Peace and Felicity

is generally a result of mutual consideration of tastes and comforts. Many discords are traceable to a disregard of this principle.

For instance, practically every man likes his bottle of beer. He would often rather drink it at home than outside.

The wise wife will note the pleasure with which he greets its appearance on the table and his enjoyment of its wholesome qualities.

Moreover, his nature benefits so that he becomes more appreciative and considerate.

Incidentally, t h e "better half" should improve her general condition and temper as the result of sharing with him a bottle or two of a beer of unusual merit.

One cannot be safer than in ordering Ballantine's Export, made in a plant famous for eighty years for brewing the choicest malt beverages. It savors of Flavor.

"Get the Three-Ring Trade-Mark."

Order from your dealer or grocer, or telephone the brewery (Market 1751).

B. ROSATI, 521 PERRY STREET
Bell Phone 1167-A.
Inter-State Phone 1584.

TRENTON EVENING TIMES (NJ) AUGUST 14, 1915

Here It Is! Fenway

5¢
EVERYWHERE

Fenway EXTRA

Raymond's Brew

The Best Glass of Ale
A Nickel Ever Bought

Because everything that is best in Malt, Hops, Water and Brewer's Skill is in Fenway.

Because Fenway preserves the Art and Honesty of old-time brewing, which, aided by the modern scientific methods, gives you a brew pleasing to the palate, agreeable to the stomach and beneficial to the entire body.

Because Fenway is the pure, healthful food beverage.

*The Brew That Boston Has Been Waiting For
Ask Your Dealer for Fenway*

Fenway BREWERIES

THE OLD McCORMICK
BREWERY CO.
BOSTON - - - - MASS.

THE BOSTON DAILY GLOBE (MASSACHUSETTS), JANUARY 4, 1915

1915

Purity—
Excellence

Superb

BOTTLED
BEER

THE
FAMILY BEER

PHONES LINCOLN 495 & 496

CHICAGO EAGLE, JANUARY 16, 1915

THE BEST
BREWING CO.

S. W. Corner Fletcher & Herndon Sts.
Tel. Lake View 110   Chicago

CHICAGO EAGLE, JANUARY 16, 1915

Harvard Bock Beer Announcement

WE TAKE pleasure in announcing that Harvard Bock Beer is now on sale.

We are not in position to claim that it is any better than the Harvard Bock Beers of previous years, for we have never spared any trouble or expense in the past in our efforts to produce a Bock Beer of the finest quality, and we feel that in this brew each year we have approached as near to perfection as possible.

In the brewing of Harvard Bock Beer we use the finest caramel malt procurable and the choicest of imported Bohemian hops.

This beer was brewed in August, 1914, so that it has already attained in our immense storage vaults an age of over six months.

It has a most delightful flavor, is full bodied and creamy, and has a rich color, for which the caramel malt is responsible, without the aid of artificial coloring.

It is a real Bock Beer of exceptional quality, and we know that it will be extremely pleasing to those who avail themselves of the opportunity of trying it.

It can be procured, either on draught or in bottles, from all dealers who endeavor to serve their patrons the best Bock Beer procurable.

HARVARD BREWING COMPANY.

Lowell, Mass.
Boston Branch,
  45 Commercial Wharf.

James R. Nicholson

President.

Harvard BOCK BEER

PREPAREDNESS

Here's proof of the value of being prepared

We are for National preparedness.

We have proved the value to any organization, whether it be government or manufacturer, of being prepared for the unexpected.

It has been an established rule of this institution to lay in our supplies of materials far in advance of their actual need.

We've done this with the Saazer Hops which we use exclusively in Budweiser, Michelob, Muenchener and our new soft drink Bevo — always a two-year advance supply. Preparedness.

During the summer of 1914, one of our officials, while on his annual hop buying trip abroad selected and purchased 275,000 lbs. (1550 bales) of the choicest Saazer Hops—and had them shipped to this country before the embargo was rigidly enforced in March, 1915—preparedness. Add this to the large stock on hand, and you will see how secure preparedness has made our position.

Our supply is sufficient to last at least until the closing days of 1918.

Preparedness pays.

Anheuser-Busch, St. Louis

George Olson & Sons

Distributors　　　　Salt Lake City, Utah

ABOVE: GOODWIN'S WEEK (UTAH)
JULY 15, 1916

RIGHT: THE HOUSTON POST (TEXAS)
MARCH 26, 1916

Moerlein's Beer Is On the Way

There's a rare treat on the rails speeding your way, friends! A carload of the famous Moerlein's Bottled Beer of Cincinnati will soon be here, on sale at the best places. Ask for

Moerlein's

FINE BOTTLED BEERS
(Bottled at Brewery Only)

Moerlein's has the mellow, delicious flavor of selected materials and of a well-aged, perfect brew. It has the snap and the healthful purity that honest quality alone can give. Order Moerlein's for home use. Order it downtown. Order by name—"MOERLEIN'S."

BERNARDO DE GEORGE, Wholesale Dealer

1403 Milam St., corner Clay Ave.　　　Phone Preston 1048.　　　Houston.

No orders solicited and no shipments made in violation of Texas laws.

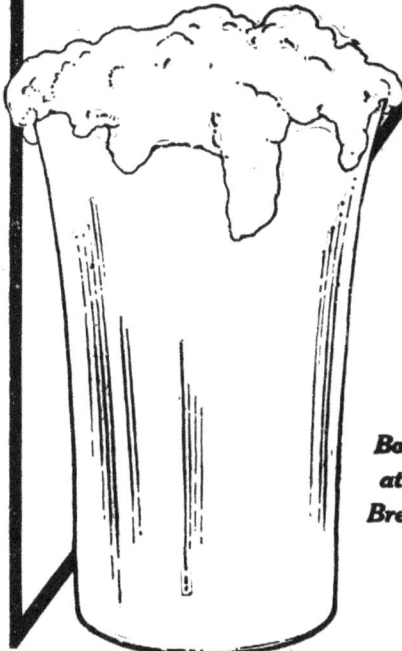

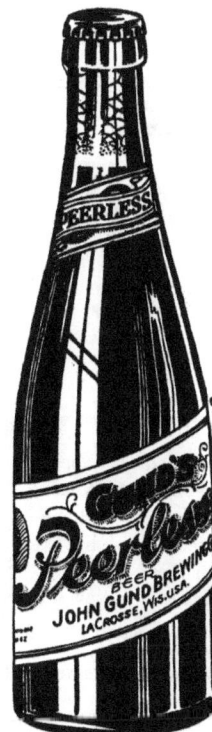

Lager Beer For Sale Here

The LIGHT of TRUTH on Heileman's Old Style Lager

Why it is so Popular

The popularity of *Heileman's Old Style Lager* is due first of all to its *pronounced* individuality of taste, quality and snappy flavor. Persons particular—accustomed to the best are the ones who continually insist upon having *Heileman's Old Style Lager*.

In the brewing of beer all prominent brewers use only the best of materials, but *it is not the material* alone which produces good beer, it's the knack of knowing how to blend the different materials to get that *snappy* taste and aromatic flavor which makes *Heileman's "Old Style Lager"* so much different from other beers, and caused it to be known as "the beer with a snap to it." *It's always uniform.*

Distribution

Heileman's Old Style Lager is now on sale from coast to coast and is the most popular beer in all localities where sold. This is best evidenced by the fact that daily *local* shipments are made as far west as Utah and as far east as New York City, Washington and Boston. Why do these people order

Heileman's Old Style Lager

and pay enormous transportation rates, when they can buy leading brands of beer at home, what's the reason? Just think this over, then try a bottle and you will know. If you don't know the name of your nearest distributor, write us as we have either a distributor or representation in the following states and all the large cities therein:

Wisconsin	Nebraska	Texas	Louisiana	Tennessee	Indiana
Minnesota	Utah	Kentucky	Florida	Illinois	Ohio
So. Dakota	Wyoming	Missouri	Virginia	Michigan	Washington, D.C.
Montana					

From the above states shipments are made into the following states: Alabama, Colorado, Georgia, Iowa, Kansas, Massachusetts, New York, Pennsylvania, North Carolina, North Dakota, Oklahoma, So. Carolina, Virginia

Porto Rico Representative, Mr. Cadierno Hermanos, San Juan

The Package

Heileman's Old Style Lager is the bottle with the green label all the way around the bottle and with the red triangle corner, reading: "None Genuine without this signature. G. Heileman Brewing Co." (the same as the corners above on bottle, only in red on a green label.) It is put up in *Crystal White Bottles* so that you can feast your eyes as well as your stomach.

G. HEILEMAN BREWING COMPANY, LA CROSSE, WIS., U.S.A.
Brewers of Heileman's Old Style Lager

Be Sure
to get the
Original and Genuine—it's

Heileman's Old Style Lager

We caution you because owing to our wonderful success the following brands have been placed on the market, so when you call for Old Style Lager see that it's Heileman's.

Old Lager
Old Tavern Beer
Old German Lager
Old German Beer
Old German Style Beer
Old Fashioned Beer
Old Settler's Beer
Old Style Select Beer
An Old Style Lager Beer
Old Style Brew
Old Style Beer
Ye Old Lager

N. C. LUDVIGSEN, Manager, Rock Island Branch
2410-2412 Third Avenue   Phone West 838
ROCK ISLAND, ILL.

NONE GENUINE without this SIGNATURE ON THE RED CORNER OF THE GREEN LABEL

Heileman Brewing Co.

> Oh Uncle Dudley!
> U-n-c-l-e D-u-d-l-e-y!
> Ma says to order another case of Burg Bräu. The other's all gone

Pure Beer is a Good Food

"It's my opinion," says Uncle Dudley, "that the proper place to serve beer is on the *family table*, where other foods are served. And that the way to *use* beer is as other foods are used—for the *good* it will do and the *strength* it will give."

Beer is now recommended by highest authorities as a *nutritious and beneficial food*, containing the flesh and blood building properties of selected cereals.

Burg Bräu

The Old German Style Lager Beer

is without a superior in *cleanliness*, *purity* and *food value*. Its matchless quality is the last word in beer excellence.

To produce a really good beer requires an intimate knowledge of both *materials* and *processes*. You can give two brewers the identical materials, and one will turn out a delicious, healthful *beer*, while the other will simply turn out a liquid.

The makers of *Burg Brau* have been thoroughly trained in the *old German way* of making beer—and the method has passed from generation to generation.

The superior quality of *Burg Brau* is secured by scientific methods of brewing and the employment of the best materials—fancy barley malt, choice Bohemian hops, and crystal spring water. Nothing but *purity* goes into it—and that purity is protected from the brewery to you.

Brewed and Bottled by

Popel-Giller Co., Inc., Warsaw, Ill.

DAILY GATE CITY & CONSTITUTION-DEMOCRAT (IOWA), SEPT 16, 1916

MANY people do not realize the food value of Ideal Beer. Do you? Do you know that Beer nourishes, soothes, livens and cleanses the body as no other beverage does? Do you know that its malt is a food partly digested and most easily assimilated?

Do you know its hops area tonic quieting to over-wrought nerves? Do you know that its small per cent of alcohol assists digestion?

Do you know that its liquid washes away clogging waste?

All These Things Are True

Your Doctor Will Tell You So!

Beer is good for both the sick and the well. Doctors prescribe it for those who are weak and "run down." The inhabitants of the most healthy and progressive nations of the world drink beer.

IDEAL IS BREWED
ONLY BY THE

CAPE BREWERY & ICE CO.

Cape Girardeau, Missouri

CAPE COUNTY HERALD (MO), JUNE 29, 1916

FOR snap and life; for full rich flavor; for Quality that insures Satisfaction, order by name that delicious beer

Moerlein's

Barbarossa

(*Bottled at Brewery Only*)

Keep a case on ice at home. Barbarossa is healthful, stimulating, cooling. Made of choicest materials, brewed by the exclusive Moerlein process, aged, sterilized.
Order a case for home.

BEARDSLEY & CO.

DISTRIBUTORS
217 Eighteenth St., Rock Island

Local and Long Distance Phone 125 R. I.

ROCK ISLAND ARGUS (IL)
AUGUST 17, 1916

Have a Good Time

It makes you a better man for the next day's work.

But take along or have sent out a case of the most delicious beer ever brewed

Moerlein's

(Bottled Only at the Brewery)

Barbarossa

Snappy, Delicious
Well-aged, Healthful

Barbarossa is the beer that everybody likes best. Phone or postal to your dealer calls a case.

Beardsley & Co.
Distributors.
217 18th St., Rock Island
Local and long distance phone 125 R. I.

ROCK ISLAND ARGUS (IL), SEPTEMBER 02, 1916

142

LEISY BEER

"The Beer Without a Headache"

This Beer, being pure, containing the best possible malt and hops, being produced after years of experience and sold with a guarantee of age and strength, is pre-eminently the beer for use on the dinner table.

No better can be obtained in any city in America and no better could be wished for by the public. Call up either phone and order a case. Once Leisy Beer is installed in the household no other will be welcome.

Order Now For July 4th

An afternoon in the woods with your friends and a few bottles of Leisy Beer would afford you more pleasure than a thousand miles of travel these hot days.

Character in Beer

LEISY IS THE HOME BEER

Leisy Beer is essentially a home beer---best for the family because of the extra precautions to make it pure. No effort, no modern machinery, no late idea is overlooked in the task of turning out an absolutely clean and good beer with no faults and no detrimental ingredients. The strengthening food qualities and rich fragrance have made Leisy Beer the best beyond question for the home.

Are You Taking Leisy's Malt-Ease?

If not commence at once, upon this, the best of all summer tonics. It is not intoxicating and is a decided health builder. Made from the choicest ingredients by the LEISY BREWING CO. Call for it at any soda fountain in Decatur.

PICNIC TIME IS HERE

LEISY ROCHESTER BEER--GREATEST OF ALL SPRING AND SUMMER DRINKS

This beer has stood the test and stands supreme for quality, purity, strength and healthfulness.

Leisy Keg or Bottled Beer can be bought at the following places: Thomas Rodgers, Ivesdale, Ill.; Frank J. Braden, Maroa, Ill.; A. N. Poli and W. T. Heindselman, Stonington, Ill., and at all leading saloons in Decatur.

FRANK H. REHLING

WHOLESALE DISTRIBUTOR.

OLD PHONE 797. NEW 759.   **802 EAST NORTH ST., DECATUR, ILL.**

THE DAILY REVIEW (DECATUR, ILLINOIS) JUNE 30, 1907

1916

THE BUTTE DAILY POST (MONTANA), OCTOBER 16, 1917

LEFT AND BOTTOM RIGHT:
GREEN BAY PRESS GAZETTE (WI)
MARCH 12, 1917

BOTTOM LEFT:
THE DAILY COURIER (PA)
MAY 8, 1917

1917

The Golden Rule

"Do unto others as you would have others do unto you"

YOU—as a voter—who would passionately assail any effort to curtail *your* liberty, have it within your power to *destroy* our business and the value of our property—and under existing conditions, deny us even the right to *ask* a jury of our own citizens to decide whether we are entitled to compensation or not.

In other words, our property can be *confiscated* and we are powerless to present our case in the courts. There is no law on the statute books of Wisconsin which gives us even the right to bring suit as other individuals and corporations may do.

Is that fair?

Is it fair that *you can demand* compensation for property losses when the losses are due to an act of the Government, State or City, while we are denied the right to *simply ask* compensation sufficient to cover the loss of our property and machinery rendered useless by your vote or the act of your accredited governmental representatives? Is it just and honest that we should be deprived of our equality of rights as decreed by the Constitution?

There is only one interpretation to equality—it means equal rights to all. We alone of all citizens and industries, paying heavily in taxes and fees toward the support of Federal and State Government, haven't the right to present in court a plea for compensation.

A State law granting to the Brewing Industry the rights that others enjoy would be in line with the Golden Rule.

The Brewers of Wisconsin

Broad Minded Physicians

Will tell you that pure, light beer from a sanitary brewery is a tonic of value

Apollo

Beer

is a healthful, mild Summer beverage

Call Bell, Main Home, Stone **10** Have the Brewery bottling delivered to your home.

DEMOCRAT AND CHRONICLE (ROCHESTER, NY), JANUARY 31, 1917

Makes A-Body Feel Like Living—

Try this good beer with your meals—and at bed-time
See how your appetite picks up!
Notice how much more you relish the things you eat!
Watch the improvement in your digestion!
That's because

Pittsburgh Brewing Co's
CONNELLSVILLE BEER

is a real health-maker! Pure, wholesome, satisfying.

Keeping Fit—

DON'T imagine that you can cure your illness with a few pills or bottles of costly medicine.

DON'T imagine that, in a few hours, you can restore the health you have neglected for months. The secret of good health and rosy cheeks is not in cure, but in prevention and in "KEEPING FIT" all the year round.

BEER, "International Health Drink," is the great internal lubricant. It assists the bodily organs to perform their normal functions and prevents illness by KEEPING the body in health.

"KEEPING FIT" is the secret of athletes of successful brain workers and of all sound and healthy persons and the secret of "KEEPING FIT" is Beer.

BEER is pre-eminently a table drink. Drink it with your meals.

SERVE
Burgmeister
COLD

Burgmeister
German Style Beverage
CONTENTS 12 FLUID OUNCES
...-GILLER CO. INC. - WARSAW ILL.

You ought to know how good it is —

and there's just one way to find out — *try it.* After that you'll be a *Burgmeister* "fan." *Burgmeister* is *good*—it can do you nothing but *good*, because nothing but *good* goes into it. Just a combination of nutritious cereals and imported Bohemian hops — made *pure*, and put up in brown bottles to *keep* it pure.

BUCK-REINER CO.,
DISTRIBUTORS
KEOKUK, IOWA
Made by Popel-Giller Co., Warsaw, Ill.

THE DAILY GATE CITY AND CONSTITUTION-DEMOCRAT (IOWA) OCTOBER 13, 1917

Why I Drink Beer

FEIGENSPAN
P.O.N.
PRIVATE SEAL BEER

"—because I've found that after the nervous tension of a day's work there is no better relaxation than a glass of good beer. The health elements contained in the barley and hops, its chief ingredients, have a soothing effect on the nerves."

Business men who take their daily drink of PRIVATE SEAL enjoy it and feel the benefit of its tonic properties. It is good and wholesome—the last drop in every bottle as good as the first. You, too, will enjoy its delicious, appetizing flavor.

PRIVATE SEAL contains the minimum of alcohol with the maximum of tonic and food value—one reason why it's "The Brew for You." Order a case from your dealer — TODAY. See that the label says P. O. N.

PRIVATE SEAL

Chr. Feigenspan
NEWARK, N.J.

The Brew for You

THE BRIDGEPORT EVENING FARMER (CT), NOVEMBER 08, 1917

Why I Drink Beer

FEIGENSPAN
P.O.N.
PRIVATE SEAL BEER

"—because beer is of the greatest value to the nursing mother. It is a wholesome, nourishing, liquid food-tonic which tones up the weakened system, restoring lost vitality and strength."

PRIVATE SEAL is skillfully brewed from the finest materials by scientific processes which retain to the fullest the natural nutritive elements. That is why physicians recommend PRIVATE SEAL to nursing mothers and all needing a food-tonic.

If you insist on PRIVATE SEAL you're sure of the best. Order a case from your dealer—TODAY—and see that the label says P. O. N.—for it's your guarantee of quality and purity.

PRIVATE SEAL

Chr. Feigenspan
NEWARK, N.J.

The Brew for You

NORWICH BULLETIN (CONNECTICUT), MAY 05, 1917

A Beverage You May Offer Your Wife

All beer is not suited for family use—"Ideal Beer"-is. It is pure, mild and wholesome—so well flavored and clean-tasting that women, as well as men, find it both refreshing and beneficial.

1917

Ideal Beer

is an appetizer, a restorative and a nutrient. Brewed and matured under ideal conditions—bottled under ideal conditions—to make an ideal beverage for home use.

"Get Acquainted" with "Ideal"—it's the kind of beer you're bound to like—and after tasting it, you'll know there's none better, purer or more wholesome. Anyway, try it once.

Your dealer will be glad to fill your order for a case of "Ideal." If he cannot supply you, 'phone Barnum 526, and we will see that you are served.

Bottled at the Brewery

THE CONNECTICUT BREWERIES CO.
BRIDGEPORT, CONN., U. S. A.

Ideal Beer

"In the Good Old Summer Time"

There is a pleasant, natural flavor about "Ideal Beer" that makes it a very refreshing and satisfying summer beverage. Pure and mild, it is most wholesome and enjoyable. Women like it, too.

"Ideal Beer" is brewed in a scrupulously clean plant, from the best ingredients to be had—and every step is constantly supervised by master-brewers. If you drink beer, "Get Acquainted" with "Ideal." You will appreciate its flavor, admire its sparkle, praise its purity. Specially brewed and bottled for home use.

Your dealer will be glad to fill your order for a case of "Ideal." If he cannot supply you, 'phone Barnum 526, and we will see that you are served.

Bottled at the Brewery

THE CONNECTICUT BREWERIES CO.
BRIDGEPORT, CONN., U. S. A.

"Get Acquainted"

Ideal Beer

Rest and Refreshment

After the work and heat of the day, an easy chair, a favorite book, and a bottle of "Ideal Beer" bring rest and refreshment to a tired man. You surely will enjoy "Ideal." It's a perfect brew of pure ingredients. Every care is taken to protect its purity, quality and flavor. The brewery bottling brings "Ideal" to you, clean and uncontaminated, with the full life and snap of "on draught" beer. It will bring you pleasure to "Get Acquainted."

Your dealer will be glad to fill your order for a case of "Ideal." If he cannot supply you, 'phone Barnum 526, and we will see that you are served.

Bottled at the Brewery

THE CONNECTICUT BREWERIES CO.
BRIDGEPORT, CONN., U. S. A.

BEER VS. WAR SUPPLIES

What a "Wet" Vote Means

The Literary Digest, One of America's Foremost Conservative Magazines, Commenting on What a Stumbling Block the Saloon is to Uncle Sam in This War, Says:

"If beer is allowed to prolong this war, causing the useless loss of many hundreds of thousands of men and many billions of money, somebody is going to pay the price once before paid by Judas Iscariot. So strongly is put the problem of civil life by publications of the Methodist church, where we see it stated—

"It will not do for us to be sixty day late or thirty days late. If we are, it will mean that the war cannot be won in 1918 and that we must stand another twelve months of agony, waste $20,000,000,000 and needlessly sacrifice the lives of 1,000,000 Americans while we're waiting for the fighting weather of 1919. . . .

"A department superintendent of one of the big tire factories in Akron, Ohio, uses sixty men in each shift. They are making gas masks, miners' respirators, and other vital war material.

"That department is working only two shifts a day instead of three because of the scarcity of labor. They pay off on Friday. On one Saturday only six of the sixty men in one shift reported for work.

"Ninety per cent of our labor troubles are due to booze,' says this superintendent. If the government would shut down on the liquor traffic we could increase our output enormously. There is no lack of labor. The only trouble is to keep it working full time."

What a "Dry" Vote Means

Now, Mr. Voter

Are you going to support the saloon and the Kaiser?

Do you want to have the German dog chase our soldiers because of the saloon and lack of supplies?

OR

Do you want to see Uncle Sam win, and bring a speedy peace to the world, and at the same time have Wilmington enjoy more prosperity, with fewer drunkards, less crime, lower taxes and happier homes?

WHICH

A "wet" city means Delay.

A "dry" Wilmington means that Delaware is going the limit in patriotism and is standing solidly, and to a man, back of Uncle Sam.

Mr. Voter, Show Your Patriotism
"VOTE DRY" November 6th

Shall Ohio Be The Booze Dump of 4 States?

Michigan—Dry by Constitutional Prohibition, going into effect May 1, 1918.

Indiana—Dry by Statutory Prohibition, going into effect April 2, 1918.

Kentucky—90% Dry and getting ready to submit a Constitutional Amendment.

West Virginia — Dry by Constitutional Amendment since 1914.

Ohio Must Protect Herself by Voting Dry

In addition to shouldering the Waste, Expense, Increased Taxes, Crime and Poverty of the Ohio Booze Business, we will have to submit to the infliction of the irreclaimable products of the Booze Business of Four States, whose undesirables will flock to the nearest Wet Dumping Ground unless we Vote Dry on November Sixth.

If there were no other reason, this one should be enough to influence the men of this State to vote Ohio Dry.

Think of the class of people to whom we would be forced to open our doors.

Think of the actual increased money cost. More police—More law machinery—More officers of the law—Higher taxes. For what? To care for More Waste, More Crime, More Poverty. More Insanity.

Ohio opens her arms to the stranger from every State and Country who comes to add to her good citizenship.

Ohio should not be forced to assume the risk and expense of caring for her neighbors Booze Products.

You can make Ohio Safe from this Undesirable Invasion by Voting Dry November 6th.

Vote Dry

THE OHIO DRY FEDERATION

J. A. WHITE, Manager

XENIA DAILY GAZETTE (OHIO), OCTOBER 25, 1917

New York Tribune

First to Last — the Truth: News · Editorials · Advertisements

TUESDAY, DECEMBER 18, 1917

Kuehlmann on Way to Join Peace Parley

Hertling Declares Just Peace With Britain Impossible

Draft Wins In Canada By Big Majority

Germans Raid British Convoy, Sink 11 Ships

House Adopts Prohibition Amendment by 282 to 128

Measure Goes to Conference—Period for Ratification Is Only Difference

Parties Evenly Divided on Vote

141 Democrats and 137 Republicans Join Independents to Vote "Yes"

Hoover Visits Wilson After Senate Rebuke

The Washington Times

FINAL EDITION

WASHINGTON, THURSDAY EVENING, JANUARY 16, 1919

PRICE TWO CENTS

WHOLE COUNTRY GOES DRY

Nebraska, Last State Needed, Ratified Prohibition Amendment Today

MAY MODIFY SECRECY OF PEACE CONFERENCE

NEWS WRITERS ARE ASKED BY PEACE ENVOYS TO GIVE VIEWS

I Ought To Be a Vampire — Mrs. Taylor Says All Her Friends Told Her So.

JAP SLAYER SHOWS HOW HARA-KIRI IS COMMITTED

States Which Ratified the Amendment

NATION WILL BE BONE DRY WITHIN YEAR FROM TODAY

SNOWDEN TO HANG, SAYS COURT

MINES REPORTED OFF VIRGINIA COAST

MRS. LEBAUDY TO BE PUT IN CELL

PRESIDENT-ELECT OF BRAZIL DEAD

Near beer and beer alternatives

With the passage of the 18th Amendment to the Constitution (Prohibition), brewers looked for other sources of revenue. By removing most or all of the alcohol from conventional beer, brewers were able to mass market a legal product labeled "cereal beverage," but almost universally known as "near beer." These beverages carried colorful names such as Bevo, Chrismo, Graino, Barlo, Bravo, Becco, Cero, Gozo, Kippo, Lux-O, Milo, and Mulo. By, 1921, production of near beer had reached over 300 million gallons a year.

Food critic Waverly Root described "near beer" as "such a wishy-washy, thin, ill-tasting, discouraging sort of slop that it might have been dreamed up by a Puritan Machiavelli with the intent of disgusting drinkers with genuine beer forever."

- From the Alcohol Policy Information System (APIS), part of the National Institute on Alcohol Abuse and Alcoholism (NIAAA)

Cool Comfort

with a bottle or two of *ice cold* Pablo. Pablo, the pure non-alcoholic thirst-quencher, is the delightful hot weather beverage because it cools and satisfies immediately. Its good old "hoppy" flavor delights and refreshes. Pablo brings invigorating comfort any time.

The Happy "HOPPY" DRINK

is the season's most popular beverage. The goodness of sparkling Pablo is more important because Pablo is healthful. Drink as much Pablo as you desire. You can't find a more enjoyable drink. Pablo chases away hot weather fatigue. Its snappy hop flavor adds zest and joy to any occasion. Keep Pablo on ice in the home—for your own use and for unexpected company Pablo gives delight and joy. By the case from your grocer or ice cold at any good drink stand.

MADE BY PABST
AT MILWAUKEE

Arkansas Grocer Company
Distributors

PABLO
NON-ALCOHOLIC

1917

In, 1917, many non-alcoholic "cereal beverages" & 'near beers' hit the market. That's when prohibition began to take hold across the country - and the United States entered World War I.

CLOCKWISE, FROM UPPER LEFT:

THE HAYTI HERALD (MO), JUNE 28, 1917

THE CLOVIS NEWS (NM), JULY 12, 1917

THE HAYTI HERALD (MO), JUNE 14, 1917

Everybody Likes PABLO
Non-Alcoholic

Pablo is *pure* and *good* and *healthful*. The snappy, invigorating flavor—the refreshment this thirst quencher gives—makes Pablo the choice of everybody who knows it.

Sparkling amber with a delightful "hop" tang—that's Pablo.

A soft drink that really satisfies.

Pablo is an invigorating thirst-quencher. You'll say so too. Try Pablo today. At any stand that sells good drinks.

Made by PABST at Milwaukee

J. M. Radford Grocery Co.
Distributors

The Happy "HOPPY" DRINK

Here Is — CERVA
The World's Best Beverage

MADE IN CERVA ST. LOUIS
This Is the Cap

Has that good, old, familiar taste of hops. And is **non-intoxicating**.

This is what you have been looking for.

Now it's here—ready for you, at all places where good drinks are sold.

This Label shows you the genuine. When you see it you know you are getting CERVA

Try A Bottle —and See For Yourself

No words can really describe CERVA But that taste will tell you what it's like. Just try a bottle—satisfy yourself.

LEMP, Manufacturers, ST. LOUIS

HAYTI ICE & COLD STORAGE CO.
HAYTI, MO.

CONTENTS 10 FL. OZ.

MADE IN ST. LOUIS
CERVA
A SOFT DRINK
SALABLE WITHOUT GOVERNMENT LICENSE
NON-INTOXICATING BEVERAGE
LEMP ST. LOUIS MANUFACTURERS

154

By 1918, traditional beer advertising was almost non-existent.

Connecticut and Rhode Island were the only two states to reject the 18th Amendment. We were able to find a few ads that appeared in Connecticut newspapers, promoting local breweries.

"I'm bringing Harry to dinner—be sure to have some 'Ideal' on ice for us!"

It's a thoughtful husband who lets his wife know when he's bringing a friend home to dinner— and it's a wise wife that is prepared for unexpected company by having on hand

Ideal Beer

"Ideal Beer" is the supreme beer for table use. Brewed, matured and bottled in the cleanest possible way, in a modern plant, by most approved methods. Even the water used is from our own artesian wells.

"Get Acquainted" with "Ideal Beer." You are sure to like its purity, mildness and flavor. It reaches your table in perfect condition.

Your dealer will be glad to fill your order for a case of "Ideal." If he cannot supply you, 'phone Barnum 526, and we will see that you are served.

"All right, Will, bring him along, we always have plenty of 'Ideal' on hand"

Bottled at the Brewery

The Connecticut Breweries Co.
Bridgeport, Conn., U. S. A.

"Get Acquainted"

Makes Good Meals Taste Better

A pure, mellow beer, served with dinner, adds to the pleasure and satisfaction of the home table. Many families appreciate and relish the quality, freshness, wholesome taste and natural flavor of

Ideal Beer

Always a fine appetizer, and an acceptable table beverage. Brewed, filtered and aged in a strictly modern and immaculately clean plant, by master-brewers, and bottled at the brewery for use in the home. "Ideal Beer" pleases particular people. "Get Acquainted."

Your dealer will be glad to fill your order for a case of "Ideal." If he cannot supply you, 'phone Barnum 526, and we will see that you are served.

Bottled at the Brewery

THE CONNECTICUT BREWERIES CO.
BRIDGEPORT, CONN., U. S. A.

1918

ABOVE: THE BRIDGEPORT TIMES
AND EVENING FARMER (CONNECTICUT)
JULY 03, 1918

LEFT: THE BRIDGEPORT TIMES
& EVENING FARMER (CONNECTICUT)
MARCH 14, 1918

With nationwide prohibition looming large on the horizon, Anheuser-Busch debuted Bevo, a non-alcoholic "cereal beverage" in 1916. It became one of the most popular "near beers," selling an estimated five million cases per year during the early, 1920s.

Demand for Bevo eventually waned, and the company stopped production in, 1929 — around the start of the Great Depression.

THE HOME OF *Bevo* THE BEVERAGE

ANHEUSER-BUSCH, ST. LOUIS.

The universal popularity of Bevo made it necessary to erect this building, the largest of its character in the world. Covers two city blocks. Floor space 26 acres. A basement 30 feet high containing 13 tracks each to accommodate ten freight cars. Will employ 2,500 people and have a bottling capacity of two million bottles daily, equal to 140 car loads, on an eight hour day basis.

THE PARISIAN (PARIS, TENNESSEE), MAY 17, 1918

Oh, So Good!

A cold bottle of **GOZO** is brimful of purity, wholesomeness and refreshment. Alone or with meals, this delicious cereal beverage means thirst satisfaction and taste contentment.

MADE AND BOTTLED BY

Gotz Co.
ST. JOSEPH, MO.

KUEHNE BROS. Topeka. Phone 300
H. D. LEE MERCANTILE CO.
Kansas City, Mo.   Salina, Kan.

THE TOPEKA STATE JOURNAL (KANSAS), MAY 31, 1918

At Last!
The Perfect Family Beverage

The world had to wait till this 20th Century for the perfect Family Beverage—a drink invigorating and nourishing with just the right sparkle and tang for a satisfying thirst quencher—that bracing, appetizing, but never habit-forming

DRY COOK'D GOLDBLUME

That new drink with the good, old, familiar taste

Every sip a tonic to tired brains and muscles. A bottle a day will keep the blues away. It's a drink to build up that growing boy, and bring him strong and robust to a splendid young manhood. The drink appropriate for every occasion.

Dry Cook's Goldblume is for sale at Soda Fountains, Drug Stores, Restaurants, Cafes, Hotels, Clubs, etc. Your Grocer will supply your household needs. Have a case sent home.

M. DEITH, Wholesale Distributor
208 East Main Street, Chattanooga, Tenn.   Phone Main 1052

THE CHATTANOOGA NEWS (TN), JUNE 21, 1918

THE TOPEKA STATE JOURNAL (KANSAS) MAY 31, 1918

1918

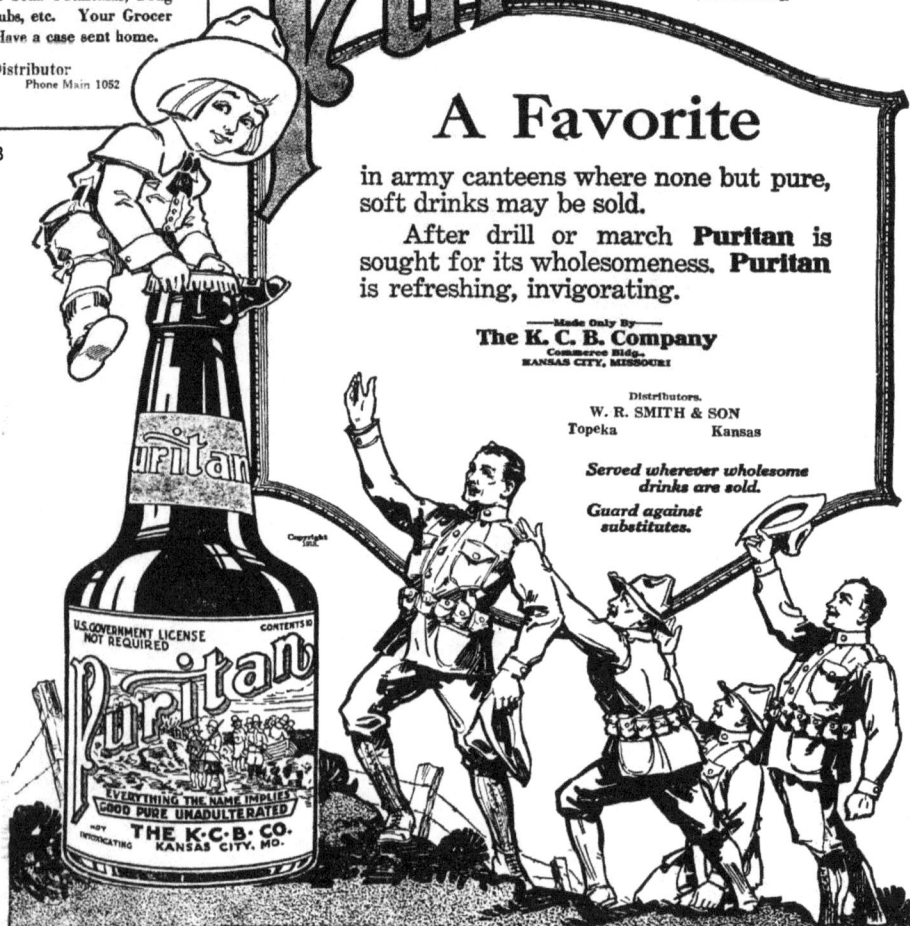

Puritan
The Unexcelled Cereal Beverage
(non-intoxicating)

A Favorite

in army canteens where none but pure, soft drinks may be sold.

After drill or march **Puritan** is sought for its wholesomeness. **Puritan** is refreshing, invigorating.

Made Only By
The K. C. B. Company
Commerce Bldg.
KANSAS CITY, MISSOURI

Distributors.
W. R. SMITH & SON
Topeka   Kansas

Served wherever wholesome drinks are sold.

Guard against substitutes.

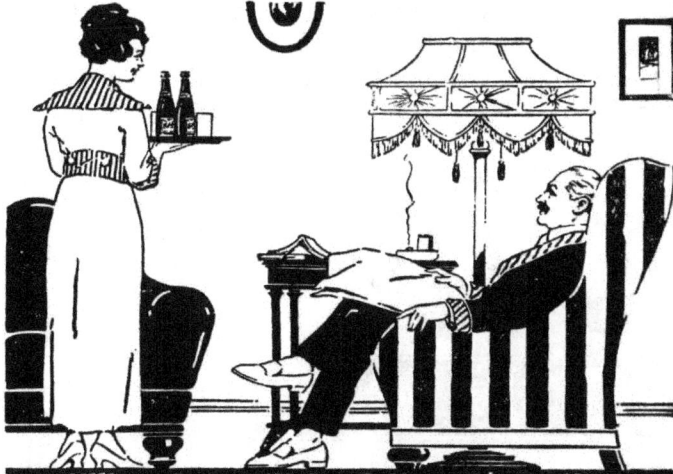

159

Coors
PURE
MALTED MILK

--and How It Originated

When Colorado went "dry" the COORS million-dollar plant at Golden ceased to operate. For a time not a wheel turned in an immense establishment representing the very latest advancements in malting methods and equipment.

Good business judgment required that this great industry be kept going—that a new product at once be found.

The range of possibilities was investigated carefully—and out of a score of likely products MALTED MILK was selected.

Because--

Malt-Making has been our principal business for nearly half a century. The founder of this company is the oldest malt-maker (in active experience) in the country. For 55 years he has been perfecting our superior process.

The quality of any malted milk depends chiefly on the malt itself—the manner in which it is prepared.

The SUPERIOR COORS process, plus our modern plant, vast experience and resources, enabled us to improve the ordinary commercial article in many ways.

COORS MALTED MILK is first of all a quality product. Its immediate success and prompt acceptance by the public are due to its COORS QUALITY.

For your convenience COORS MALTED MILK is put up in sealed half-pound, one-pound and five-pound jars. Your druggist is now carrying COORS, or can easily obtain it for you.

The better-class soda fountains are serving COORS. Ask the dispenser to make you "A COORS MALTED MILK." We know you will be pleased—for COORS is *better*.

The Adolph Coors B. & M. Co.
Makers of Malt since '73.
Denver and Golden, Colorado

Omaha Office—918 Farnum St.
(Telephone Douglas 3086.)
This is the first of a series of ads telling you about Coors Malted Milk.

Coors
PURE
MALTED MILK
SELECT BRAND

PRICE $1.00

The Mark of Quality in Malt Products for 44 Years.

The Professor Says:

"Bartels Bock Beer

Is Now Ready"

This is the Bock Beer season, and our special brew this year is just as good as the best we have ever produced which means that it is the BEST BOCK BEER BREWED. On draught or in bottles.

Ask for it.   Phone for it.

THE PROFESSOR SAYS:

"There has never been any other beverage, as popular as beer, Bartels Beer is brewed and bottled with the utmost care and is so low in alcoholic content as to make it practically a temperance drink."

PERFECTION BEER

Brewed with great skill, from the best barley and hops procurable, it is clear, rich and mellow, a beverage of unmistakable high quality.

HOWELL & KING CO.

Pittston, Pa.   Both Phones

161

Schlitz FAMO
is more than a drink

It is a food. Every time you take a glass of Schlitz Famo you are taking something to eat.

Every compound essential to the human body is present in Schlitz Famo—protein, carbohydrates, mineral matter and water—the only factor absent being fats, and they are formed in the body from the carbohydrates.

These elements repair and build up broken-down tissues and impart to the body heat and muscular energy.

That's why we say Schlitz Famo is a *worth-while* cereal beverage.

It is non-intoxicating. It is healthful, refreshing and satisfying. It has the wonderful hop aroma.

On sale wherever soft drinks are sold. Order a case from

Schlitz

Telephone Randolph 1380
E. A. Saunders' Sons' Co.
14th and Cary Streets
Richmond, Va.

Made Milwaukee Famous

RICHMOND TIMES-DISPATCH (VIRGINIA), MAY 08, 1919

Lily

A CEREAL BEVERAGE

"THE EMBLEM OF PURITY

The Whole Family Knows _Lily_ Is Healthy and Refreshing

Lily is a beneficial beverage that lead them all in popularity with men, women and children It's tasty—it's refreshing—it's likeable—it's satisfying. It's pleasing aroma and taste makes it an enjoyable drink for every purpose—also a cooler to serve with meals or luncheon.

This non-alcoholic drink is made by

The Rock Island Brewing Co.

EQUAL to the BEST BEER _Lily_

—_Tastes the same and is as pure as its name_

THE IDEAL SUMMER DRINK

Ask for _Lily_ _at your favorite place._ _Have a case of it in your home_ _Keep a bottle or so in your place of business._ _Try it today—you'll endorse it—you'll recommend it._

| Price $1.70 two dozen | Telephone R. I. 88 and 889 | Empties to be returned |

ABOVE:
ROCK ISLAND ARGUS.
(ILLINOIS)
JUNE 20, 1919

LEFT: SOUTH BEND
NEWS-TIMES
(INDIANA)
JUNE 22, 1919

THE NEW

Silver Edge

BREW

"Get the Hoppy Taste"

Ask your friends to join you in a bottle of Silver Edge or Bock Brew. They are the drinks of good fellowship and good cheer. Made from the best hops and barley malt by master brewers and properly flavored. They are the summer drinks without a fault. You really should have a case in the house.

IN CRYSTAL CLEAR BOTTLES

THE MUESSEL BEV. CO.   BOTH PHONES

1919

The Narragansett Brewing Company Announces

The New Brew   the Old Name

"Gansett"

TRADE MARK
REG. U. S. PAT. OFF.

NON-INTOXICATING

THE production of this modern drink marks the climax of years of experience in the making of pure food brews. The same care and skill which have made the name "Narragansett" a synonym of quality in beers and ales are employed in the making of the new brew, GANSETT.

In every glass you will recognize the tang of hops and the rich flavor of choicest malt, due to the skillful use of best ingredients thoroly brewed and aged, and delivered to you in sterilized, hermetically sealed bottles.

The sparkling effervescence pleases the eye and gives life to the drink.

Order in cafes, hotels, restaurants and clubs.

Ask your dealer to deliver a case to your home.

If your dealer cannot supply you, write or phone the

NARRAGANSETT BREWING CO.
PROVIDENCE,   RHODE ISLAND

NORWICH BULLETIN (CONNECTICUT), SEPTEMBER 25, 1919

164

Smile--Smile--Smile

THE new "Hoosier Cream" helps to make the world a more cheerful place to live in. It pleases the eye with its inviting snap and sparkle. Its tasty tang of tonic hops delights the palate and is a treat for thirsty throats. It is delicious, nutritious, and satisfying, with unusual power to refresh, revive, and invigorate. It is a drink that is as pure and wholesome as sunshine, as cooling as ocean breezes.

Hoosier Cream
An Oasis in the Desert of Thirst

"Hoosier Cream" is served at hotels, cafes and soda fountains---insist on having it served cold---Ice cold.

Delivered to your home in cases of dozen bottles by your grocer or by

Hoosier Cream Company
South Bend   Indiana

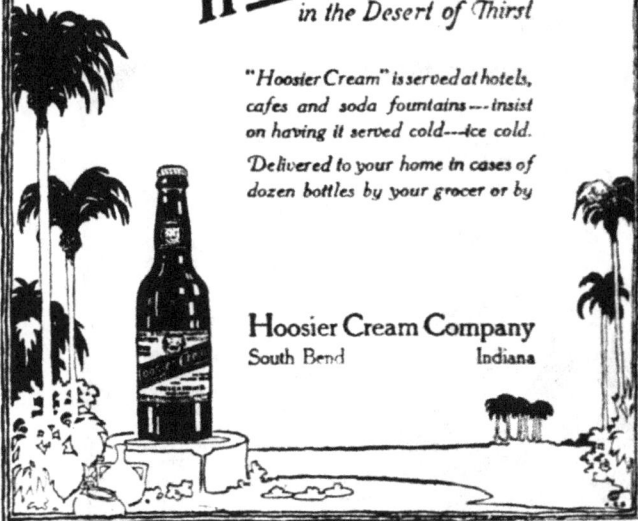

SOUTH BEND NEWS-TIMES (INDIANA), JUNE 22, 1919

Lots of Beverages

will give you a measure of satisfaction; try New Style Lager and get the very highest degree of satisfaction.

HEILEMAN'S
New Style Lager
Is Snappy—

This is due to the use of only the purest of ingredients and the perfect blending of same.

It possesses a tang and after taste all its own, is refreshing, wholesome, nourishing and is a particular brew for particular people.

It's the real merit—the genuine snappy flavor that is responsible for the unprecedented demand for New Style Lager. Its taste is its point of excellence because it is famous for its snappy taste. You'll always insist upon it if you try it.

G. HEILEMAN COMPANY,
La Crosse, Wisconsin, U. S. A.

New Style Lager
Beverage Co.
Distributors

Bismarck, N. D.

THE BISMARCK TRIBUNE (ND), JUNE 17, 1919

165

ABOVE:
THE BISMARCK TRIBUNE (NORTH DAKOTA)
AUGUST 05, 1919

RIGHT TOP:
GREAT FALLS DAILY TRIBUNE (MONTANA)
JULY 03, 1919

RIGHT BOTTOM:
GREAT FALLS DAILY TRIBUNE (MONTANA)
JULY 30, 1919

Announcing
the Re-creation
of
ANHEUSER-BUSCH'S FAMOUS
Budweiser

IT is the fixed policy of Anheuser-Busch to comply with every provision of public laws and regulations. That policy will be adhered to in the future as in the past. In view of the Act of Congress, effective October 29, 1919, we feel that our many friends and customers have the right to know how the Anheuser-Busch industrial plants will be utilized.

Our greater development plans include, among other new products, an additional cereal beverage to which we shall apply our well-known trade-name Budweiser. This beverage will be manufactured, in every detail, according to our original Budweiser process, and de-alcoholized to conform to Federal law. It will possess the genuine Budweiser flavor and quality.

Budweiser, re-created, will be manufactured from the choicest, most wholesome and nutritious cereals—and hops, noted for their tonic effects. It will be fully and maturely lagered, put up in sterilized, hermetically sealed, 12-ounce brown bottles, and pasteurized to insure its permanent purity and quality.

We guarantee that this Budweiser is bacteria free, will keep in any climate, and is healthful and nutritious.

We shall be ready to begin shipments by January 1, 1920.

Budweiser is manufactured and bottled exclusively at the plant of

ANHEUSER-BUSCH, ST. LOUIS, U.S.A.

HEALTH

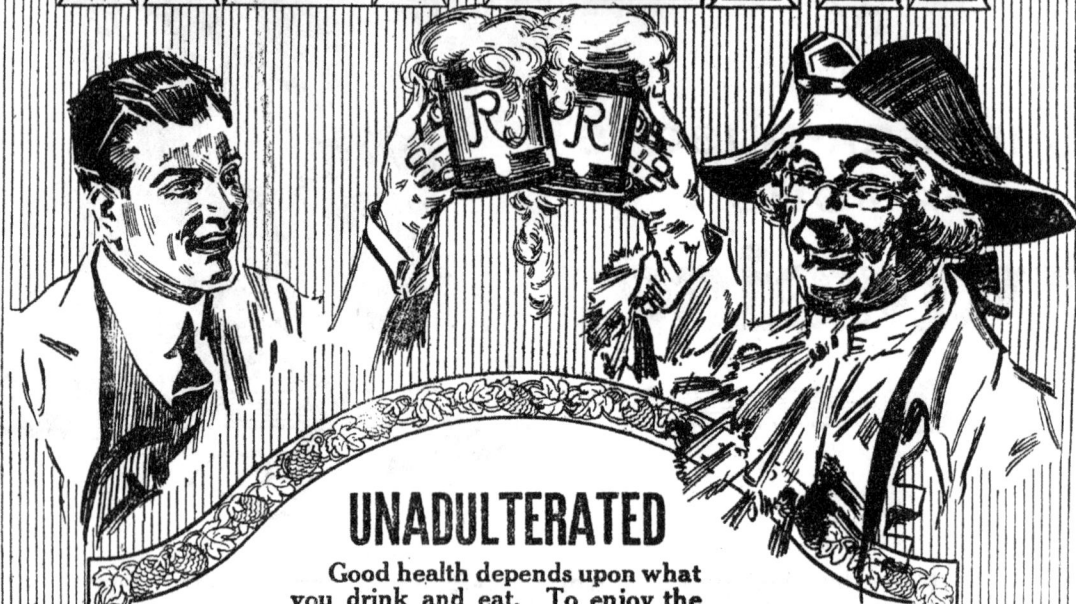

UNADULTERATED

Good health depends upon what you drink and eat. To enjoy the best of health you must select pure liquids and pure foods. Any family physician will so advise.

When it comes to selecting a pure, unadulterated, invigorating drink containing a little alcoholic substance, every Chemist who knows anything about a good wholesome brew will tell you that one of the best that was ever brewed is

JACOB RUPPERT'S
Knickerbocker
The Brew That Satisfies

Knickerbocker is a genuine brewery product containing all the best that can possibly be extracted from pure hop and barley malt. It is aged and matured in the same vessels and by the same methods that made it justly famous years ago.

Knickerbocker is a pasteurized brew. Every drop of water used in the making is filtered, every vessel and bottle is sterilized; otherwise the brew could not be classed as a genuine, unadulterated brewery product.

FOR SALE EVERYWHERE

JACOB RUPPERT
Third Avenue, 90th to 92nd Street

ALBUQUERQUE MORNING JOURNAL (NM), JUNE 25, 1921

THE FAYETTE FALCON, SEPTEMBER 16, 1921

THE BISMARCK TRIBUNE (ND), JULY 09, 1921

Happy Days, Folks!
this canny Scotch Brew

THIS is to offer you a taste of the Good Old Days. A supreme Brew that we've brought over from Scotland. It's an old-time formula—not a prohibition makeshift. For it dates back to 1740—over one hundred and seventy years.

All the exhilaration, the mild stimulation. *But within the law.* That's the story, men. Now give it a trial.

We Didn't Count The Cost

We've been trying to do something like it ever since the Eighteenth Amendment.

We called in the experience of brewers of world repute. Expense was disregarded.

We were willing to wait until we could offer you, as a beer lover, not a "near beer"—flat, no thrill—but a brew that you would enjoy just as much as any you ever drank during the good old days.

For the first time in this country, we now offer you a drink—Old Scotch Brew—a formula unchanged for nearly two centuries—but within the law.

Not a "near beer," friends, but a perfect brew.

You Won't Believe Us

We know you'll be skeptical. We were, too.

3,000 NEW YORK PHYSICIANS SAY

"Drink It For Health"

They drink Old Scotch Brew themselves and prescribe it for their patients. Millions of bottles have already been consumed in New York City alone. And every day this average jumps ahead in great leaps.

For we've been brewers more than seventy years. And two years ago, we wouldn't have believed what's been done with this Scotch Brew was even a wild possibility.

Neither Would 200 Old-Time Beer Drinkers

When the first brew was properly complete, we put it to the supreme test. Sent a supply to five groups, each of 200—old-time beer drinkers; customers of ours in the open days.

They had told us it couldn't be done. That Pilsner richness with all its malt and hop fragrance was only a memory. But they came. They tasted. And then they went after it!

Ninety-eight per cent agreed we had attained it. Most, that we had surpassed it.

All the smoothness — the exhilaration — but within the law.

Most Talked Of Drink in New York

Wherever you go, whether it is in the finest hotels, the exclusive country clubs, the noted restaurants, or the finest grocers and delicatessens, you will find Good Old Scotch Brew.

Give it a whirl today. See what the Scotch—the canny Old Scotch—have done for beer lovers.

That good old, wholesome richness—and stimulus—is here again, but within the law.

The drink for hot days and parched throats. A reminder of the old times. There's a surprise for you in the perfect blending of rich malt and hops. And that Pilsener flavor invites you to "have another." Good Old Scotch Brew is served and sold everywhere. Let's cheer for the auld Scots. They gave us Good Old Scotch Brew.

Names Worth Reading

Here are some of the representative dealers who sell Good Old Scotch Brew. You can get it in every section of the Metropolis. Order your case of Good Old Scotch Brew today—for the thirsty, hot days to come.

"We found it in Scotland, men"
You can find it at—

GOOD OLD SCOTCH BREW
MADE IN THE U.S.A. by
S. LIEBMANN'S SONS, INC.
NEW YORK
UNDER FORMULA & LICENSE OF
JAMES AITKEN & CO.
BREW. & CO.
FALKIRK, SCOTLAND
FOUNDED 1740
CONTAINS LESS THAN ½ OF 1% ALCOHOL BY VOLUME · CONTAINS 12 FLUID OUNCES

THE WEATHER
East Texas: Cloudy, local showers in south and east portions, colder tonight; Wednesday partly cloudy preceded by showers on coast, colder in south and east.
Thermometer Readings

Corsicana Daily Sun

FULL LEASED WIRE ASSOCIATED PRESS SERVICE

CORSICANA, TEXAS, TUESDAY, DECEMBER 5, 1933.—TWELVE PAGES

VOL. XXXVI, NO. 6.

PRICE FIVE CENTS

LOCAL MARKETS

PROHIBITION ENDS LATE TODAY

LONG FORCES ARE COMPLETELY ROUTED IN THREE PARISHES

NO ELECTION HELD IN NUMEROUS DISTRICTS; LIGHT VOTE ELSEWHERE

BATON ROUGE, La.

Threatened Champ

PRELIMINARY TAX REVISION PROGRAM IS RECOMMENDED

WIDE CHANGES IN RATES ARE SUGGESTED BY HOUSE COMMITTEE TUESDAY

THE RIDE'S ON UNCLE SAM

TEXAS LAWS STILL PROHIBIT SALE OF HIGH-POWER LIQUOR

ONLY BEER OF NOT MORE THAN 3.2 ALCOHOLIC CONTENT LEGAL IN STATE

Triumphed in Debut

LAW TRIED ALMOST FOURTEEN YEARS AND ADJUDGED WANTING

THIRTY-SIXTH STATE, UTAH, EXPECTED RATIFY AMENDMENT LATE TODAY

Ironwood Daily Globe

VOLUME 15, NUMBER 14.

ASSOCIATED PRESS LEASED WIRE-TOWN SERVICE

IRONWOOD, MICHIGAN, TUESDAY EVENING, DECEMBER 5, 1933.

10 PAGES

SINGLE COPY 5 CENTS

"FORTUNE KNOCKS BUT ONCE:" BUT MISFORTUNE DROPS IN FREQUENTLY.

PROHIBITION ERA IS ENDED

State Store Plan Returned to Bill

REPEAL FINDS MICHIGAN DRY

Senate Committee Hopes to Release Bill to Floor Today.

NAME KATAJA JURY AT NOON

Four Women and Eight Men Selected to Hear Murder Trial Today.

FIVE PLEAS OF GUILTY

A jury of four women and eight men had been selected at noon today to determine the guilt or innocence of Toivo Kataja of De Pere.

ARMED CITIZENS DEFY ELECTION

State Police Sent to Set Up Ballot Boxes, Avoid Bloodshed.

EARLY BALLOTING LIGHT

Baton Rouge, La., Dec. 5—With defiant and heavily armed citizens patrolling major highways and polling places on block plans.

Utah Is 36th State To Ratify Repeal

Government May Release Medicinal Liquor Stocks

Washington, Dec. 5—The government is considering a plan to release all medicinal liquor stocks for beverage purposes immediately.

One official said that in all likelihood the plan would be approved late in the day. The Utah action is expected about 9:30 Eastern Standard Time.

PENNSYLVANIA, OHIO ACT TODAY

American People Now Face

Latest Happenings
HOME EDITION
Of World Events

Pharos LOGANSPORT Tribune

YOUR HOME TOWN NEWSPAPER

VOLUME 89.

FOR ALL DEPARTMENTS PHONE 119

PHAROS-TRIBUNE, LOGANSPORT, INDIANA, TUESDAY EVENING, DECEMBER 5, 1933

ALL LEADING MARKETS PUBLISHED DAILY

MEMBER A. B. C.

More than
50,000 READERS
See Your Ads Daily

HOUR OF REPEAL NEARS

Pennsylvania And Ohio Ratify 21st Amendment

Thirty-four
Thirty-fi...
Take Fo...

WEATHER FORECAST
OHIO: CLOUDY AND colder tonight, possibly rain. Wednesday fair.

PROHIBITION IN OHIO LASTED 5,453 DAYS

THE PIQUA DAILY CALL CITY EDITION

51st. YEAR   No. 41

PIQUA, OHIO, TUESDAY, DECEMBER 5, 1933

PRICE THREE CENTS

OHIO CONVENTION VOTES FOR REPEAL OF THE 18TH AMENDMENT AT SESSION HELD TUESDAY AFTERNOON

WEATHER FORECAST
UTAH—Fair Wednesday; unsettled in northwest.
IDAHO—Rain or snow Wednesday, Thursday.
WYOMING, NEVADA—Cloudy Wednesday, Thursday.

The Salt Lake Tribune

VOL. 128, NO. 53.

Entered at the postoffice at Salt Lake City as Second-Class Matter

SALT LAKE CITY, UTAH, WEDNESDAY MORNING, DECEMBER 6, 1933.

22 PAGES—FIVE CENTS

LOCAL METAL PRICES
Gold (newly mined) $34.01
Silver 43½c
Lead 4.15c
Copper 8.05c
Zinc 4.90c
Local Weekly Settlement Prices
Lead ...... .41c   Copper 7.45c

UTAH VOTE ENDS PROHIBITION ERA

Delegates to the Utah constitutional convention, liquor problem to the several states. Left to right: Thurman, L. B. Hampton, Mrs. John A. Hendricks, Keyser, secretary.

1933

New York's "Gay White Way" celebrates emancipation of John Barleycorn

LOGANSPORT PHAROS TRIBUNE (INDIANA), DECEMBER 6, 1933

REPEAL SHIFTS THE SCENES

Exit, Prohibition . . . As Curtain Falls On Nation's 13-Year Experiment

CORSICANA DAILY SUN (TEXAS), DECEMBER 5, 1933

New Yorkers Rush To Buy Legal Liquor

Shortage of Whisky Seen As Thousands Crowd Warehouses

By DALE HARRISON

NEW YORK, Dec. 7 (AP)—Business was popping around town today with all the pep of a cork from a bottle of champagne.

Activity at liquor warehouses made the places look like the bleacher entrance to the Polo Grounds at a world series game.

Wine and liquor stores were so busy that one of them had to call the police to disperse customers at closing time.

Smart hotels were gleefully reporting record business. Some, despite large stocks of liquor, found their supplies near exhaustion even before cocktail hour yesterday.

Drivers of liquor trucks worked as long as 24 hours at a stretch tired but glad. One wine firm had made deliveries of 16,000 cases early today and was still far behind in filling orders.

Department stores selling liquor found their aisles packed like a rush-hour subway train. Most of customers asked for rye, but if there was no more rye they took gin; and if no gin, then brandy. The demand for wines was sur-

(Continued on Page Seven)

ANSWERING CRY OF 'BOTTOMS UP'

1933

Out of the west came this message: "Utah ratifies repeal", and the prohibition era in the United States came to an end early Tuesday evening. "Bottoms up" was the echo throughout the county to Utah's message and the three pretty celebrants in the top photo were quite willing to obey the command at a bar in New York. Bottom picture shows Chicago celebrating the end of prohibition.

CLOCKWISE FROM UPPER LEFT:

RENO GAZETTE (NV), DEC 22 1933
LUDINGTON DAILY NEWS (MI), DEC 16 1933
EVENING REPORT (PA) DEC 14 1933
PORTSMOUTH HERALD (NH), DEC 6 1933
RENO GAZETTE (NV), DEC 5 1933

Index

Beer brands & breweries in this book

Like this book? We have others!

For more old-fashioned fun, look for...

Vintage Homes: Adult Coloring Book: Luxurious Victorian Houses & Mansions
Vintage Women: Adult Coloring Book series
and
Something Old: Vintage Wedding Dress Fashion Look Book

Other Synchronista titles:
All-In-One Pregnancy Calendar, Daily Countdown, Planner & Journal
Motivation & Mandalas Adult Coloring Book
Book of Brilliant Things Activity Book
Large Print Word Search Puzzles series
.... and others

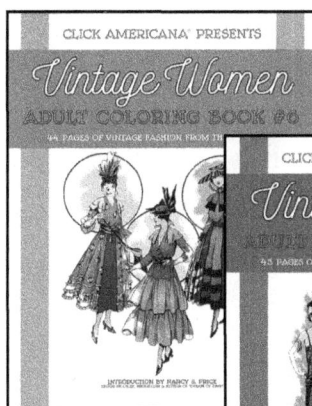

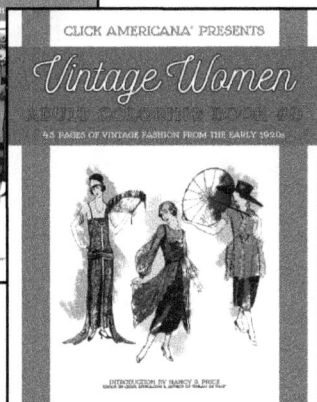

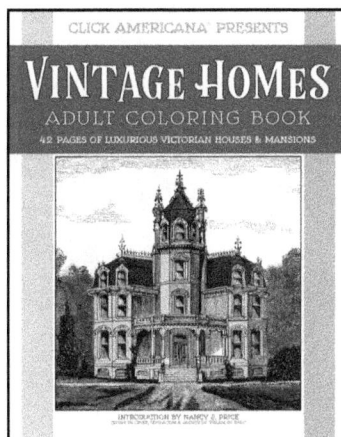

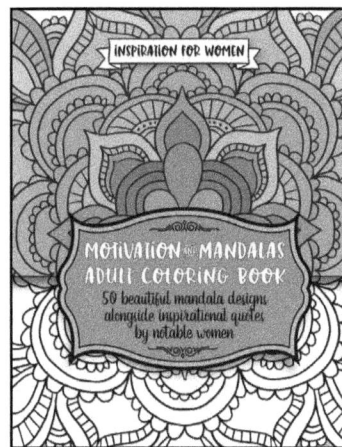

Check out our websites, too...

ClickAmericana.com
Thousands of articles, photos and vintage ads
from throughout American history.

Myria.com
Smart stuff for real life:
Health, parenting, psychology,
science, tech, entertainment — plus
recipes, home decor & other good things.

The End